D0941449

D 742 G7 C5597
C.02
3 0450 00045 7342

Winston Churchill's

SECRET SESSION SPEECHES

Compiled and with introductory notes

by CHARLES EADE, editor of *The Sunday Dispatch*

19  46

Simon and Schuster, New York

PUBLISHED BY SIMON AND SCHUSTER, INC.
ROCKEFELLER CENTER, 1230 SIXTH AVENUE
NEW YORK 20, N. Y.

MANUFACTURED IN THE UNITED STATES OF AMERICA
AMERICAN BOOK–STRATFORD PRESS, INC., NEW YORK

CONTENTS

Introduction

MR. WINSTON CHURCHILL made five speeches of major importance in Secret Sessions of the House of Commons during the war. In accordance with Parliamentary custom, these speeches were not recorded even for official and historical purposes.

Fortunately, the speeches were of such character that Mr. Churchill, before delivering four of them, prepared full texts of what he proposed to say. This precaution was made necessary by the fact that, in order to ensure complete accuracy and avoid any breaches of security, the speeches were checked by the Service Departments and other interested ministries before they were delivered.

These notes remained in Mr. Churchill's possession when he resigned the premiership. When the government which succeeded his ministry lifted the ban on revealing what had occurred at the Secret Sessions, Mr. Churchill gave me his notes and authority to compile them into this volume. The speeches delivered on June 25, 1941, April 23, 1942, and December 10, 1942, have already been released to the press. The others are published here for the first time.

It is impossible to guarantee that the speeches as now printed are a completely accurate, word-for-word report of what Mr. Churchill said in Secret Session. It is likely that he occasionally changed words and phrases to suit the mood and temper of the House, but such alterations must have been only of a minor character. Unquestionably, the speeches printed in the following pages are a complete and exact record of what Mr. Churchill intended to say, and it is unlikely that he varied them to any great extent.

They form a necessary contribution to the history of the war and explain many events which were puzzling at the time.

Acknowledgment is expressed of the courtesy of the American authorities concerned for permission to publish the documents quoted.

CHARLES EADE

THE FALL OF FRANCE

ON JUNE 19, 1940, the Prime Minister made a full statement to the House of Commons upon the situation created by the impending collapse of French resistance. He concluded with the words: "Let us therefore brace ourselves to our duties, and so bear ourselves that, if the British Empire and its Commonwealth last for a thousand years, men will still say, 'This was their finest hour.'"

After a few speeches the House went into Secret Session and the debate continued during the rest of that day and through the whole of the next day, June 20, when the French government, headed by Marshal Pétain, had actually sought armistice terms from Germany and Italy. As the Prime Minister's statement had been made on a motion for the adjournment, he had the right of replying on the general debate. When he rose in the House on the evening of June 20 to wind up the debate in Secret Session, he held nine pages of typewritten notes and headings, on which he had written additions and alterations as the discussion proceeded. There is no full record of the speech he delivered. The other Secret Session speeches printed here were dictated beforehand and every argument and phrase carefully considered and checked. As this debating speech lasted more *than an hour, and as the occasion was tragic and critical in the extreme, the following nine pages, with photographed reproductions of the notes he used, are of interest.*

They show that he told the House he considered a Secret Session should be a normal part of its procedure and not necessarily associated with a crisis. He warned his listeners that it would be folly to underrate the gravity of the impending German attack but felt that, so far as the air raids were concerned, the people of Britain would get used to them. The enemy, he added, were not using their bombers very cleverly and our own bombing was far more effective.

Mr. Churchill then discussed the Allies' military errors and failures on the Continent and the melancholy position of the new French government. He expressed his confidence in the strength of Britain's resisting power and added that, if Hitler failed to invade or destroy Britain, he had lost the war. "If we get through the next three months," he wrote in his notes, "we get through the next three years!"

He spoke of America's attitude to the war and emphasized that nothing would stir them so much as the news of fighting in England. He added: "The heroic struggle of Britain is the best chance of bringing them in."

Mr. Churchill concluded by speaking of the formation of the new government headed by himself and said he had a right to depend on loyalty to his administration and to feel that we had only one enemy to face—"The foul foe who threatens our freedom and our life and bars the upward march of man."

BRITAIN FIGHTS ALONE

Notes on a speech to the

House of Commons

June 20, 1940

Secret Session. House of Commons.

My reliance on it as an instrument for wagin
wa

More active and direct part for its Members
L.D.V.

All this in accordance with past history.

This S.S. a model of discretion.

My view always Govt. strengthened by S.S.

~~Quite ready to have others.~~

Agree with idea S.S. shd be quite a normal p
of our procedure,
not associated with any crisis.

Relief to be able to talk without enemy read

Quite ready to have other S.Ss.,
especially on precise subjects.

But I hope not press Ministers engaged in
conduct of war too hard.

Mood of the House.
Cool and robust.

Speeches most informative.
Difficult to betray any secrets disclosed
toda

oore-Brab (Wallesey) Praise.

e was sorry I mentioned expert advisers
favoured fighting on.

oliticians and Generals, -

n last war and this.

ot put too much on the politicians:
even they may err.

oering. How do you class him?
He was an airman turned politician.

like him better as an airman.
Not very much anyway.

oore-Brab tells us of his wonderful brain,
and the vast dictatorial powers and plans.

nyhow he did not produce the best pilots
or the best machines,
or perhaps, as we may see presently,
the best Science.

M.B. said 250 nights in the year
when no defence against night bombing.

~~I hope it is not so~~

This is one of those things you can only tell
by finding out.

We have had a couple of nights of bombing,
evidently much worse than that.

Folly underrate gravity attack impending.

But if 100 to 150 bombers employed
entitled to remark:

Not very cleverly employed.

Hardly paid expenses.

Learn to get used to it.
Eels get used to skinning.

Steady continuous bombing,
probably rising to great intensity
occasionall
must be regular condition of our lif

The utmost importance preserve morale of
people,
especially in the night work of factorie

A test of our nerve against theirs.

Our bombing incomparably superior.
More precise, and so far more effective.

Indiscriminate bombing v. selected target

Enemy have a great preponderance numbers.
but their industry
much more concentrated.

o one can tell result.

his supreme battle depends upon
the courage of the ordinary man and woman.

hatever happens, keep a stiff upper lip.

uty of all M.Ps. to uphold confidence
and speed production.

ellinger's speech.

ailure of French war conception.

he Maginot line. The defensive theory.
Brilliant military achievement of Hitler.
Triumph of the offensive spirit.

riumph of long-prepared machinery.

riginal strategic failure
advance into Belgium
without making sure of the sub-
Maginot line,

and without having a strategic reserve
to plug a gap.

ate of Northern Armies sealed when
the G. armoured Divisions curled round
their whole communication.
Abbeville, Boulogne, Calais.

ot 2 days' food.
only ammunition one battle.

Question of forming Torres-Vedras line.

Quite impossible with Air attack on ports.
One in three supply ships sunk.
all experience shows [illegible]
Situation looked terrible,
especially when Belgium gave in.

Give all credit to all three Forces.

Army fought its way back;
Navy showed its wonderful reserve power;
Air Force rendered naval work possible.

B.E.F. a fine Army. Only 10 Divisions

Without proper armoured Divisions
~~or a~~ well-equipped,
but placed in a hopeless
strategic situation.

Much to be thankful for.

Melancholy position of the French Govt.

We have to make the best of them.

No criticisms, no recriminations.
We cannot afford it, in public.

Petain. Reynaud. Darlan.

5 precious days largely wasted.

Surprise if mercy shown by Germany.

The French Fleet. The French Empire.
Our policy.

Urge them to continue
but all depends upon the battle of Britain

I have good confidence.

Some remarks about Home Defence.

Belisha spoke of 'man the defences
and resist the enemy.'

That will play its part;
but essence of defence of Britain
is to attack the landed enemy at once,

leap at his throat
and keep the grip until the life is out
of him.

e have a powerful Army
growing in strength and equipment
every day.

any very fine Divisions.
~~Mobile Brigades~~

igilant coast watch. Strong defence of
ports and inlets.
obile Brigades acting on interior lines
Good prospects of winning a victory

[illegible] [illegible]

Quantity and quality [illegible] ~~[illegible]~~

If Hitler fails to invade
or destroy Britain
he has lost the war.

I do not consider only the severities
of the winter in Europe.

I look to superiority in Air power
in the future.

Transatlantic reinforcements.

If get through next 3 months
get through next 3 years.

It may well be our fine Armies
have not said goodbye to the Continent
of Europe.

If enemy coastline extends from the Arctic
to the Mediterranean

and we retain sea-power
and a growing Air power

it is evident that Hitler
master of a starving, agonized and
surging Europe;

will have his dangers as well as we.

ut all depends upon winning this battle
here in Britain, now this summer.

f we do, the prospects of the future
will expand,

and we may look forward
and make our plans for 1941 and 1942

and that is what we are doing.

ttitude of United States.
Nothing will stir them like fighting
in England.

lo good suggesting we are down and out.

he heroic struggle of Britain
best chance of bringing them in.

nyhow they have promised fullest aid
in materials, munitions.

tribute to Roosevelt.

ll depends upon our resolute bearing
and holding out until Election issues
are settled there.

If we can do so, I cannot doubt
a whole English-speaking world
will be in line together

~~and with all the Continents except Europe~~
and with the Oceans and with the Air
and all the Continents except Europe
(RUSSIA)

I do not see why we should not find our way through
this time, as we did last.

Question of Ireland.
Greatly influenced by a great Army developing here.

Germans would fight in Ireland
under great disadvantages.

Much rather they break Irish neutrality than we.

Lastly, say a word about ourselves.

How the new Govt. was formed.

Tell the story Chamberlain's actions.

Imperative there should be loyalty, union
among men who have joined hands.

Otherwise no means of standing
the shocks and strains which are coming

I have a right to depend loyalty
to the administration
and feel we have only one enemy to face
the foul foe who ~~menace~~ threatens
our freedom and our life,
and bars the upward march of man.

THE BATTLE OF BRITAIN

ON TUESDAY, September 17, 1940, while German bombers raided London unceasingly throughout the night, the House of Commons went into Secret Session to hear from Mr. Winston Churchill how Parliament would carry on with its duties during the Battle of Britain and in face of the heavy bombardment from the air which was going to be inflicted on the capital during the months ahead.

The notes used by Mr. Churchill on that occasion were, fortunately, so full as to form an almost exact record of what he said. After explaining why the dates of sittings would be kept secret and the hours altered, Mr. Churchill warned the House of the ever-growing dangers of an invasion attempt. He revealed that upwards of seventeen hundred self-propelled barges and more than two hundred seagoing ships were already gathered at ports in German occupation. He rejected any thought that these preparations might be only pretense and said that some of these vessels, when bombed by the RAF, had blown up with tremendous explosions, showing that they were fully loaded with all the munitions needed for the invading armies.

Despite all these threats and perils, the Prime Minister ended by assuring his listeners that he was "as sure as the sun will rise tomorrow" that Britain would be victorious.

PARLIAMENT IN THE AIR RAIDS

A statement to the

House of Commons

September 17, 1940

THE REASON why I asked the House to go into Secret Session was not because I had anything particularly secret or momentous to say. It was only because there are some things which it is better for us to talk over among ourselves than when we are overheard by the Germans. I wish to speak about the sittings of the House and how we are to discharge our Parliamentary duties.

A few days ago I had a notification from the Chiefs of the Staff. They considered that the date and time of this meeting of ours today had been so widely advertised that to hold it would be to incur an undue risk, and that it should be put off to some date and hour which had not been publicly announced. I felt, however, that Members would be offended if any course was taken which suggested for a moment that we should shirk our duty out of considerations of personal safety. And then there is all that argument which occurs to everyone of our setting an example, and of the incongruity of our ordering government departments, and urging factory workers to remain at work, while we ourselves did not assemble on particular occasions as we had resolved to do. Moreover, the rules of the House are such that we could only have avoided meeting at this hour by an earlier meeting on Monday, which would alter the hour, and a Monday meeting would have caused much inconvenience under the present conditions of travel.

I, therefore, took the responsibility of disregarding the very well-meant warning which we had received from those charged with the technical burden of national defense.

Nevertheless, this is a matter on which there should be clear thinking. We should fail in our duty if we went to the other extreme, and in a spirit of mettlesome bravado made it unduly easy for the enemy to inflict loss and inconvenience upon the public service. We ought not to flatter ourselves by imagining that we are irreplaceable, but at the same time it cannot be denied that two or three hundred by-elections would be a quite needless complication of our affairs at this particular juncture. Moreover, I suppose that if Hitler made a clean sweep of the Houses of Parliament it would give widespread and unwholesome satisfaction throughout Germany, and be vaunted as another triumph for the Nazi system of government. We must exercise reasonable prudence and a certain amount of guile in combatting the malice of the enemy. It is no part of good sense to proclaim the hour and dates of our meetings long beforehand.

There are two kinds of air risks, the general and the particular. The general risk in air raids is largely negligible. It is at least a thousand to one. But the risk of staying in a particular building which the enemy undoubtedly regards as a military objective is of a different order. Here, we are sitting on the target. This group of well-known, prominent buildings and towers between three major railway stations, with the river as a perfect guide by night and day, is the easiest of all targets, and I have very little doubt that they will need extensive repairs before very long. We have seen how unscrupulous and spiteful the enemy is by his daylight attacks on Buckingham Palace. And anyone has only to walk to Smith Square or St. Thomas's Hospital to see the kind of damage that a single airplane can do. We have not got to think only of ourselves in considering the matter. There is a large number of officials and staff attached to the House who have to be in attendance upon us when we are sitting. This building itself is not well constructed to withstand aerial bombardment. There is an immense amount of glass about the place, and the passages are long and narrow before the blast- and splinter-proof shelters can be reached. There is no certain defense against the attacks which might so easily be made. There is no guarantee that the warning will be given in time. Even our watcher up aloft would very likely give his signal only at the moment when the bombs were already released. The firing of the artillery is no useful warning because it fires so often, and we should be hindered in our business if we attended to that.

If we are to do our duty properly we ought to adapt our arrangements to the peculiar conditions under which we live. Therefore, I am going to propose to the House three measures which they will find fully consonant with their dignity and with their duty, and with your permission, Mr. Speaker, I now propose to outline their character.

The first is that the hours and dates of our sittings shall not be made public in the press or announced beforehand, and that they shall be lapped in uncertainty. This is a very considerable protection, because it removes a large part of the incentive to the enemy. If we are not known to be gathered here, a large part of the attractiveness of the Palace of Westminster as a target will be gone, and we may have the use of the building and its conveniences for a longer period than is otherwise possible. Therefore, I propose to move that when we adjourn today it will be to an hour and a date which will as far as possible be kept secret. The date should evidently be tomorrow, because it is inconvenient for Members to come from all over the country under present conditions merely for a single day's sitting.

But the second measure which I propose is that we should alter the hours of our sittings. We must expect that at any time after dark the nightly air raiding will begin. Our barrage will be firing, and apart from bombs, great numbers of shell splinters, usually described most erroneously as shrapnel, will be falling in the streets. It is better for Members and the officials and staff of the House to be in their homes or in their shelters before this begins. I shall therefore propose that we meet at eleven in the morning, and conclude our business at four in the afternoon, with half an hour for the debate on the adjournment.

This brings me to my third proposal. The fact that we meet in the mornings will be a great convenience to Members, but it only throws a heavier burden on Ministers and the Public Departments. Not only Cabinets but many scores of important meetings take place every morning, and the whole work of the staffs and the departments in the afternoon is affected by their decisions. If any large number of Ministers have to be in attendance upon the House, the whole progress of War Administration will be delayed or even deranged. Take the case of the Minister of Health, who is tomorrow to be in charge of a debate upon the general health of the nation. That is a most interesting and important topic. But the Minister of Health is already working to the utmost limit of his strength on the many difficult situations created by the bombing of London; by its effects on drainage, which is a serious problem, some of our great sewers having been broken; upon the rehousing of persons rendered homeless through their dwellings being destroyed or damaged, or because they have to be evacuated from districts on account of unexploded bombs or other special causes. He has also to deal with the dangers to national health arising out of people being crowded together in shelters, and contracting diseases which under these conditions, unless they are vigorously coped with, may foster epidemics of diphtheria, typhoid, and influenza. In fact, he is fighting the danger of pestilence.

Now, I am first of all a Parliamentarian and House of

Commons man. If I have any say in matters at the present time, it is due mainly to this House, and I therefore set Parliamentary duties above everything, subject, of course, to the leave of the House, which I am sure would be generously given. My right honorable friend will therefore carry out the program as it has been arranged if the House so desires. But I must appeal to the House to show its consideration for Ministers and for a government in whom it has recorded its confidence almost unanimously. We are really doing our very best. There are no doubt many mistakes and shortcomings. A lot of things are done none too well. Some things that ought to be done have not yet been done. Some things have been done that had better have been left undone. But looking broadly at the whole picture as it is viewed by any impartial eye, the way in which our system of government and society is standing up to its present ordeals, which will certainly increase in severity, constitutes a magnificent achievement, and has justly commanded the wonder and admiration of every friendly nation in the world. I ask, therefore, for the indulgence of the House, and for its support in not requiring too many sittings in the next month or two. I shall propose when we adjourn on Thursday that we adjourn until Tuesday, October 15. We shall, of course, meet a good deal earlier, but the House will be asked to leave the exact date unspecified and to be proposed by me as Leader of the House to Mr. Speaker, giving sufficient notice to Members for their convenience. Of course, if anything happens which raises any novel or fundamental issue, for which the authority of Parliament is required, we shall immediately summon Parliament even if it were only a few days after we have separated, and we shall make it our business to keep in touch with all parties and groups, not only through what are called "the usual channels," but through any other channels which may be open.

Some ignorant people suppose that Members of Parliament are only doing their duty when they are sitting in this Chamber, either making or listening to speeches. But surely at this time of all others, Members not otherwise occupied in national service may do invaluable work in their own constituencies. This is especially true of constituencies which have been knocked about by the enemy's fire, and where the people will have need of having their representative among them to share their dangers, resolve their perplexities, and, if it were ever necessary, uphold their spirit.

These next few weeks are grave and anxious. I said just now in the Public Session that the deployment of the enemy's invasion preparations and the assembly of his ships and barges are steadily proceeding, and that at any moment a major assault may be launched upon this island. I now say in secret that upwards of seventeen hundred self-propelled barges and more than two hundred seagoing ships, some very large ships, are already gathered at the many invasion ports in German occupation. If this is all a pretense and stratagem to pin us down here, it has been executed with surprising thoroughness and on a gigantic scale. Some of these ships and barges, when struck by our bombing counterattack and preventive attack, have blown up with tremendous explosions, showing that they are fully loaded with all the munitions needed for the invading armies and to beat us down and subjugate us utterly. The shipping available and now assembled is sufficient to carry in one voyage nearly *half* a million men. We should, of course, expect to drown a great many on the way over, and to destroy a large proportion of their vessels. But when you reflect upon the many points from which they could start, and upon the fact that even the most likely sector of invasion, i.e., the sector in which enemy fighter support is available for their bombers and dive bombers, extending from the Wash to the Isle of Wight, is nearly as long as the whole front in France from the Alps to the sea, and also upon the dangers of fog or artificial fog, one must expect many lodgments or attempted lodgments to be made on our island simultaneously. These we shall hope to deal with as they occur, and also to cut off the supply across the sea by which the enemy will seek to nourish his lodgments.

The difficulties of the invader are not ended when he sets foot on shore. A new chapter of perils opens upon him. I am confident that we shall succeed in defeating and largely destroying this most tremendous onslaught by which we are now threatened, and anyhow, whatever happens, we will all go down fighting to the end. I feel as sure as the sun will rise tomorrow that we shall be victorious. But I ask the House to assist us in solving these problems, worse than any that have ever threatened a civilized community before, by meeting the wishes of the government in the arrangement of Parliamentary business and in lightening the burden which rests upon the men in charge.

Formal resolutions in accordance with what I have said will be proposed to the House for their approval this afternoon while the House is still in Secret Session.

THE SHIPPING SITUATION

On Wednesday, *June 25, 1941—the day the German and Russian armies clashed in the first big battle of the Eastern tront—the House of Commons went into Secret Session to hear one of the gravest statements made by Mr. Churchill during his premiership—a frank, unvarnished report on the shipping situation and the war against the U-boats.*

Before delivering this momentous speech, on a problem which threatened the very survival of the British people, the Prime Minister committed to paper a full record of what he intended to say. The Service Departments checked his statement for statistical accuracy and security, and it is certain that Mr. Churchill adhered almost exactly to the text printed in the following pages.

During his speech he read the directive he had issued, as Minister of Defense, for the vigorous prosecution of the "Battle of the Atlantic," and he revealed that in the previous twelve months 4,600,000 tons of Allied shipping had been sunk. This was a speech of grim, unpleasant facts and of difficulties being successfully overcome. It had a calming effect on critics of the government.

THE BATTLE OF THE ATLANTIC

A speech to the

House of Commons

June 25, 1941

FROM THE beginning of the war to the end of 1940 the losses of British, Allied, and neutral merchant shipping from all causes amounted to about five million tons. But after allowing for our new building and the capture, purchase, and chartering of foreign vessels, the total amount of shipping serving us at the end of 1940 was only about one and a half million tons less than in peacetime. The total tonnage serving us at the outbreak of war can be variously estimated from twenty-six millions to about twenty-two millions, according to the classes of shipping included. Not all this tonnage, it is true, is available for importing service. Some four millions have been withdrawn for naval and military purposes. Some vessels are engaged in essential Empire trade; some are too small to cross the Atlantic; some are immobilized by damage. Tankers amounting to some four and one-half millions form a specialized class wholly absorbed by our oil requirements. We hope to maintain our oil imports fairly near the prewar level, and in the figures which I shall presently give you for imports I shall therefore exclude oil. If the losses I have quoted are compared with the total fleet, they would amount to about five per cent. On so large a turnover that could not be considered dangerous for sixteen months of the kind of war we have been fighting.

There were, however, two important aggravations. First, there was no comparable windfall to set against the continuance in 1941 of losses at the rate sustained in 1940. Secondly, the protective measures of the Admiralty—convoy, diversion, degaussing, mine clearance, the closing of the Mediterranean, generally the lengthening of the voyages in time and distance, to all of which must be added delays at the ports through enemy action and the blackout—have reduced the operative fertility of our shipping to an extent even more serious than the actual loss. The Admiralty naturally think first of bringing the ships safely to port and judge their success by a minimum of sinkings. But the life and war effort of the country also depend directly upon the weight of imports safely landed.

In the best peace year we imported about sixty million tons. After France went out we could not look forward to an import in 1941 of much more than half this total. Since I went to the Admiralty at the beginning of the war, I have formed and developed a strong Statistical Department of my own under Professor Lindemann. In this way I receive every week a number of key diagrams which cover the entire field of our war effort, and reveal graphically all unfavorable or favorable tendencies. The increasing discrepancy between the comparatively small net loss of tonnage and the enormous fall in imports became more and more evident during the winter of 1940. Many measures were taken by the departments principally concerned, the Ministry of Supply, the Ministry of Food, and the Board of Trade. The imports had for some time past been strictly controlled and all luxuries had been eliminated. The programs of these three importing departments were framed so as to give priority to articles which make the least demand on shipping space. Our export trade was concentrated on articles of a high exchange value. Ships were increasingly concentrated upon the short Atlantic haul. Drastic steps were taken to stimulate home production. I will not enter upon the question of home production of food, for that requires a debate of its own. But great savings have been made in the imports of timber, which stood at over ten million tons at the beginning of the war, at four and one-half million tons in 1940, and has at last been reduced for the current year to little more than one million tons, reduction being made good partly by economies, and partly by home felling, which has been done on a very large scale. Oil reserves have fallen from the high level at the beginning of the war; but our stocks in all essentials of raw materials have been maintained, and the food reserves stand this summer higher than they did a year ago. At the end of September, when the new harvest is in, they will be substantially better than when the first war harvest was garnered.

I must, however, try to bring home to the House the extraordinary difficulties of our strategic position arising from Hitler's mastery of the European coast. These difficulties far exceed anything that was experienced in the last war. In fact, if at the beginning of 1940 we had been told that the enemy would be in effectual command of all the Continental Atlantic ports, from Narvik to Bayonne, most of the high naval and air experts would have said that the problem of supplying Britain would become insoluble and hopeless.

I remember that in the last war an inquiry was made into the possibilities of feeding this island if the Port of London were closed, and the report was extremely pessimistic. The Port of London has now been reduced to one-quarter. The traffic of all the ports on the east coast is enormously shrunken. The traffic along the south coast is at a tithe of its normal. The English Channel, like the North Sea, is under the close air attack of the enemy. We have had to transfer our importing capacity increasingly to the west-coast ports, and as Southern Ireland is denied us as a base for our protecting flotillas and air squadrons, practically the whole of our traffic comes in through the North Western Approaches between Ireland and Scotland, and is handled at the Clyde, the Mersey, and to a lesser extent at the ports of the Bristol Channel. All these ports are under frequent and sometimes long-repeated air attacks, and apart from the damage, there are all the restrictions caused by air-raid damage, delays, and blackout conditions.

During the winter months the U-boats developed a new technique of attacking by night. The losses mounted heavily, and the new year dawned upon us bleak and grim.

Besides the depredations of the U-boats, there was growing up a form of air attack upon our Western Approaches by means of long-range Focke Wulf machines. These aircraft—of which happily at the beginning there were only a few, but which might be expected to grow constantly in numbers—could sally out from Brest or Bordeaux, fly right round the British islands, refuel in Norway, and then make the return journey next day. On their way they would see far below them the very large convoys of fifty or sixty ships, to which we have been forced to resort through the scarcity of escorts. Moving inwards or outwards on their voyages, they could attack these convoys or individual ships with destructive bombs, or they could signal by modern perfected wireless to the waiting U-boats, advising them what course to steer in order to make interceptions.

The U-boats themselves could maneuver on the surface in the darkness at a greater speed than the convoys. By somewhat reducing the war heads of their torpedoes and somewhat increasing the compressed air bottle which drives them, they were able to fire volleys of torpedoes which ran through the array of the convoys, sometimes striking three or four ships at once. I went through as a Minister some of the worst periods of the U-boat attack in the last war. I have studied the conditions long and carefully, and have thought often about them in the intervening years. Nothing that happened then, nothing that we imagined in the interval, however alarming it seemed at the time, was comparable to the dangers and difficulties which now beset us. I repeat that every high authority that I know of, if asked in cold blood a year ago how we should get through, would have found it impossible to give a favorable answer. I have no doubt that the able experts who advise Hitler told him that our doom was certain.

We do not hear much about the mining now, yet almost every night thirty or forty enemy airplanes are casting these destructive engines in all the most likely spots to catch our shipping. We do not hear about it much because by the resources of British science and British organization it has been largely mastered. We do not hear much about it because twenty thousand men and a thousand ships toil ceaselessly with many strange varieties of apparatus to clear the ports and channels each morning of the deadly deposits of the night. We do not hear much about this work or about the men who do it or the men who plan it. It is taken as a matter of course, like the heroic, marvelous feats of the Salvage Service, which has recovered since the war, in every circumstance of storm and difficulty, upwards of a million tons of shipping, which would otherwise have been castaway. A few critical or scathing speeches, a stream of articles in the newspapers, showing how badly the war is managed and how incompetent are those who bear the responsibility—these obtain the fullest publicity; but the marvelous services of seamanship and devotion, and the organization behind them, which prove at every stage and step the soundness of our national life; the inconquerable, the inexhaustible adaptiveness and ingenuity of the British mind; the iron, unyielding, unwearying tenacity of the British character, by which we live, by which alone we can be saved, and by which we shall certainly be saved—and save the world—these, though fully realized by our foes abroad, are sometimes overlooked by our friends at home.

But I must go back to the beginning of the present year. In January Hitler made a speech threatening us with ruin and pointing with confidence to that combination of air and sea power lapping us about on all sides, by which he hoped, and still hopes, to bring about our starvation and surrender.

"*In the spring*," he said, "our U-boat war will begin at sea, and they will notice that we have not been sleeping [shouts and cheers]. And the Air Force will play its part and the entire armed forces will force the decision by hook or by crook."

Early in January, as the House will remember, we formed the Import Executive, consisting of the principal importing departments under the Chairmanship of the Minister of Supply, and its sister executive, the Production Executive, under the Ministry of Labor. The principal object of the first of these bodies was to grapple with the import situation, to improve the organization of shipping and transport, and to solve the many intricate problems of labor and organization arising at the ports. There was also the division of our imports between the different importing departments to be settled.

At the beginning of March, after a heavy batch of sinkings, I thought it right to proclaim "The Battle of the Atlantic." I did this in order to focus the extreme attention and energies of all concerned upon this struggle for life, and to meet the increased severity of attack which Hitler threatened. I am going to read to the House, as we are in Secret Session, the actual directive which I issued, and which, with the approval of the War Cabinet, was issued on March 6 to all concerned. This is, of course, a most secret document and should on no account be quoted or referred to.

THE BATTLE OF THE ATLANTIC

Directive by the Minister of Defense

In view of various German statements, we must assume that the Battle of the Atlantic has begun.

The next four months should enable us to defeat the attempt to strangle our food supplies and our connection with the United States. For this purpose—

1. We must take the offensive against the U-boat and the Focke Wulf wherever we can and whenever we can. The U-boat at sea must be hunted, the U-boat in the building yard or in dock must be bombed. The Focke Wulf, and other bombers employed against our shipping, must be attacked in the air and in their nests.
2. Extreme priority will be given to fitting out ships to catapult, or otherwise launch, fighter aircraft against bombers attacking our shipping. Proposals should be made within a week.
3. All the measures approved and now in train for the concentrations of the main strength of the Coastal Command upon the North Western Approaches, and their assistance on the east coast by Fighter and Bomber Commands, will be pressed forward. It may be hoped that, with the growing daylight and the new routes to be followed, the U-boat menace will soon be reduced. All the more important is it

that the Focke Wulf, and, if it comes, the Ju-88, should be effectively grappled with.

4. In view of the great need for larger numbers of escorting destroyers, it is for consideration whether the American destroyers now in service should go into dock for their second scale of improvements until the critical period of this new battle has been passed.
5. The Admiralty will re-examine, in conjunction with the Ministry of Shipping, the question of liberating from convoys ships between thirteen and twelve knots, and also whether this might not be tried experimentally for a while.
6. The Admiralty will have the first claim on all the short-range AA guns, UP weapons and PACs that they can mount upon suitable merchant ships plying in the danger zone. Already two hundred Bofors or their equivalents have been ordered to be made available by ADGB and the factories. But these should be followed by a constant flow of guns, together with crews or nucleus crews, as and when they can be taken over by the Admiralty. A program for three months should be made.
7. We must be ready to meet concentrated air attacks on the ports on which we specially rely (Mersey, Clyde, and Bristol Channel). They must therefore be provided with a maximum defense. A report of what is being done should be made in a week.
8. A concerted attack by all departments involved must be made upon the immense mass of damaged shipping now accumulated in our ports. By the end of June this mass must be reduced by not less than four hundred thousand tons net. For this purpose, a short view may for the time being be taken both on merchant and naval shipbuilding. Labor should be transferred from new merchant shipbuilding which cannot finish before September, 1941, to repairs. The Admiralty have undertaken to provide from long-distance projects of warship building or warship repairs up to five

thousand men at the earliest moment, and another five thousand should be transferred from long-distance merchant shipbuilding.

9. Every form of simplification and acceleration of repairs and degaussing, even at some risk, must be applied in order to reduce the terrible slowness of the turn-round of ships in British ports. A saving of fifteen days in this process would in itself be equivalent to five million tons of imports, or a tonnage of one and one-quarter millions of the importing fleet saved. The Admiralty have already instructed their officers in all ports to aid this process, in which is involved the process of repairs, to the utmost. Further injunctions should be given from time to time, and the port officers should be asked to report what they have done and whether they have any recommendations to make. It might be desirable to have a conference of port officers, where all difficulties could be exposed and ideas interchanged.

10. The Minister of Labor has achieved agreement in his conference with employers and employed about the interchangeability of labor at the ports. This should result in a substantially effective addition to the total labor force. In one way or another, at least another forty thousand men must be drawn into ship-repairing, shipbuilding, and dock labor at the earliest moment. Strong propaganda should be run locally at the ports and yards, in order that all engaged may realize the vital consequences of their work. At the same time, it is not desirable that the press or the broadcast should be used unduly, since this would only encourage the enemy to further exertions.

11. The Ministry of Transport will ensure that there is no congestion at the quays, and that all goods landed are immediately removed. For this purpose, the Minister will ask the Chairman of the Import Executive for any further assistance required. He should also report weekly to the Import Executive upon the progress made in improving the ports on

which we specially rely by transference of cranes, etc., from other ports. He should also report on the progress made in preparing new facilities at minor ports, and whether further use can be made of lighterage to have more rapid loading or unloading.

12. A Standing Committee has been set up of representatives from the Admiralty Transport Department, the Ministry of Shipping, and the Ministry of Transport, which will meet daily and report all hitches or difficulties encountered to the Chairman of the Import Executive. The Import Executive will concert the whole of these measures and report upon them to me every week, in order that I may seek Cabinet authority for any further steps.
13. In addition to what is being done at home, every effort must be made to ensure a rapid turn-round at ports abroad. All concerned should receive special instructions on this point, and should be asked to report on the measures which they are taking to implement these instructions, and on any difficulties that may be encountered.

In order to follow this matter with the closest personal attention, and to give directions from day to day which clear away difficulties and obstructions, and force action upon the great number of departments and branches involved, I held a weekly meeting at which all the Ministers and many of the high functionaries concerned were present, both from the Fighting Services and on the civil side. At these meetings, of which there have been twelve, each lasting some two and one-half hours, the whole field was gone over, and everything thrashed out. Thus, nothing was held up for want of decisions. Presently Mr. Harriman, President Roosevelt's expediter of supplies, joined us and made his own invaluable contribution from the American end. These meetings reinforced the work of the Import Executive, and now as things have begun to run more smoothly, I have felt it possible to make the meetings fortnightly.

I was assisted in my work not only by Professor Lindemann's Statistical Department, but also by the Cabinet Secretariat. These two bodies analyzed the weekly reports which came in from all departments, and directed my attention to the weak points and shortcomings. I tell the House all this because I am not sure that there is much good in long strings of complaints and criticism, in themselves often both well founded and well meant, made by Members who are quite unaware of the remedial steps which have been taken, in many cases long before they got to know of the evils. To have debates filled with all this when no comprehensive reply can be made without exposing to the enemy the whole of our inside arrangements, misgivings, and corrective measures is neither a healthy nor a helpful process. Presently I will show the House what have been the results of our exertions up to date.

Meanwhile there is another aspect which must be considered. All our war policy, the whole scale and maintenance of our armies abroad, the movement to the east of thirty or forty thousand men a month, as well as the conditions of life to be undergone by the people of this island—all this depends upon the tonnage imported and the number of ships we have afloat on the seas. We have, in fact, to make a budget of imports for the year 1941 exactly in the same way as the Chancellor of the Exchequer makes his Financial Budget for the year. By the end of March, all the studies and discussions of our ways and means were completed. In my capacity as Minister of Defense, I submitted to the War Cabinet my proposals for the size and character of the three branches of the Fighting Services, and also the quantity and character of the imports for which we should strive.

I will read the House the memorandum which sets forth what we hope to achieve in the present year, so far as imports are concerned. Here again I am going to read the actual words of my memorandum of March 26, because I am anxious to take the House fully into the confidence of the government. But I must again emphasize that the figures in this memorandum should not on any account be made public. In this way I shall answer the reproaches which are made here and out-of-doors that we are complacent and lacking in foresight and that there is no concerted plan which all departments are following.

As to complacency, let me say this. Do not let anyone suppose that inside this enormous government we are a mutual-admiration society. I do not think, and my colleagues will bear me witness, any expression of scorn or severity which I have heard used by our critics has come anywhere near the language I have been myself accustomed to use, not only orally, but in a continued stream of written minutes. In fact, I wonder that a great many of my colleagues are on speaking terms with me. They would not be if I had not complained of and criticized all evenly and alike. But, bound together as we are by a common purpose, the men who have joined hands in this affair put up with a lot, and I hope they will put up with a lot more. It is the duty of the Prime Minister to use the power which Parliament and the nation have given him to drive others, and in war like this that power has to be used irrespective of anyone's feelings. If we win, nobody will care. If we lose, there will be nobody to care.

Now I come to my memorandum of March 26:

We should assume an import of not less than thirty-one million tons in 1941. On this basis, food cannot be cut lower than fifteen million tons, and a million is required for the Board of Trade. This leaves fifteen millions for the Ministry of Supply, as against nineteen millions to which they were working on the thirty-five million program. A cut of four millions has, therefore, to be made by the Ministry of Supply, for which a revised program should be framed. Ferrous materials, timber, and pulp seem to offer the main field of reduction. As we can now buy steel freely in the United States, the keeping in being of the whole of the existing steel industry cannot be accepted as an indispensable factor. We must try to import in the most concentrated forms and over the shortest routes. This principle must also influence food imports.

Should our total imports fall below thirty-one millions, the deficit should for the present be met by the Ministry of Food and the Ministry of Supply on the basis of one ton cut in food to two tons in supply. Should the imports exceed thirty-one millions, the benefit will be shared in the same proportion. The position will be reviewed in the autumn, when this year's harvest is known.

The Ministries of Food and Agriculture should, upon the basis of fifteen million tons import in 1941, concert an eighteen months' program, drawing as may be necessary upon our meat reserves on the hoof to cover the next six months, but endeavoring to provide by concentrated imports the most varied dietary possible for the nation at war. By taking a period as long as eighteen months, it should be possible to avoid hurried changes in policy, to use preserves as balancing factors, and to make the best use of the assigned tonnage.

This program requires an adjustment of our fighting forces. The air power will continue to be developed to the utmost within the limits fixed by import tonnage, and with the present priorities and assignments. The Admiralty ship building programs have been remodeled so as to ensure for the time being a pull forward of construction likely to be available in the present year, at the expense of long-term policies which, however necessary, must yield their priorities till we are through the present crisis. I had to make very severe demands upon the War Office, first to cut down their manpower requirement, and secondly to feed their growing formations by internal economies, in order, among other things, to provide for a very much larger proportion of armored divisions and of the more highly technical units for which our increasing supply of modern weapons would be forthcoming.

The size and scale of our armies is wrapped in mystery, and I am not going to give any precise figure. I wish, however, here in secret, to correct exaggerated ideas. People talk of armies of four or five millions. If the Germans believe it, so much the better. Do not let us reassure them. In fact, however, the actual size is only about half the figure I mentioned. In addition, there is, however, the Home Guard of one and three-quarter millions and the Dominions, Indian, and Colonial armies, which are large and important and for which we provide many essential services.

In order to adjust the War Office need for manpower to the possibilities of tonnage, to the requirements of the Air Force and the Navy, and to the vast sphere of munition production, I had to ask my right honorable friend the Secretary of State for War and the Army Council to accept a reduction of just under half a million men. They did so, and have recast their organization accordingly. But having done that, I must warn the House that I cannot and will not have the Army drained, mulcted, and knocked about any further. They will help in emergencies, but otherwise the soldiers must not be taken from their training. In a few months or even less we may be exposed to the most frightful invasion that the world has ever seen. We have a foe who, to wipe us out forever, would not hesitate to lose a million men; and if he tries to come we have got to take care that he loses that or better. For this purpose, military training must be carried to the highest degree. The men must be active, well disciplined, competent with their arms, practiced in all the latest maneuvers which our hard experience suggests. We cannot have men pulled out of their units, disturbing symmetry and order, on any large scale for any purpose.

The coal problem has been mentioned, and strenuous efforts are being made to solve it. Unless these efforts are successful, we shall have to shiver this winter. But it will be better to do that than starve our munition factories, or pull fifty thousand miners out of the Army. They are grand fighting men, these miners, and I am only sorry we cannot allow any more to exchange the pick for the rifle, as they would be proud to do. I am satisfied that up to the present a good layout of our available forces has been made. But, of course, later on in the year, we must review the position. I have hopes that the growing ascendancy and power of our Air Force, and the ever-improving methods of night defense against air raiders, may enable us to get a further reinforcement for the Army to meet the normal wastage, apart from battle casualties, by a very considerable scrubbing of ADGB (Air Defense of Great Britain), which now claims nearly half a million men. One hundred seventy thousand women are needed, and, if found, will liberate a corresponding number of men from the batteries, searchlights, and predictors. There are any amount of tasks of the highest importance and honor which women can do in ADGB, fighting alongside their menfolk under the fire of the enemy.

Now let me return to the shipping and tonnage problem, and let us see what are the results which have followed from my directive of March 6 and from the ceaseless efforts of all my colleagues in this field and along these lines. The sixteenth report of the Select Committee on National Expenditure, which was issued last week, bears witness to the fact that a considerable improvement in the conditions of the ports has already been effected (see paragraph 4). No one can, however, be satisfied with conditions as they are. Much more remains to be done, and much more must be done, if this part of our problem is to be solved. There could be no better subject for a public debate than the matter contained in this searching and well-balanced report. But I did not wish that debate to take place until the House had been put in possession of our general scheme and outlook, and could judge everything in its proper setting. A debate on what is called production could very well be centered around this report, and should also of course extend to the conditions prevailing in the mines and factories.

I take first the operational side. Three hundred Bofors and 100 H S guns have been installed in merchant ships and crews provided by the War Office to work them. Many hundred machine guns with other weapons of new types have also been mounted. A large scheme was instituted to improve the merchant seamen in the use of these weapons. Specially fitted omnibuses are provided in which practical training and instruction can be given. This is now beginning to yield results. The powerful reinforcements of long-range aircraft—the Hudsons and the Whitleys—which were sent in March and April to the Western Approaches are now active. We have received from the United States and have converted here for fighting purposes a considerable and growing number of those splendid long-range flying boats, the Catalinas, to aid our own Sunderland aircraft. It was a Catalina that first spotted the *Bismarck*. A number of special vessels carrying catapult Hurricane aircraft are employed on patrolling duties, and a much larger number of merchant ships are being fitted to carry one Hurricane each on their ordinary commercial voyages. The first of these are just beginning to come back with the convoys from the other side of the ocean. Soon every North Atlantic convoy or its escort will contain at least one vessel carrying a catapult fighter aircraft which can rise to attack, with very hopeful prospects, a prowling Focke Wulf.

New airfields in Northern Ireland, in the Hebrides, and in Iceland are being constructed with all possible speed. Iceland is a point of particular importance, and I hope to have more to tell you about this one of these days. Of course, up to the present only an installment of these new measures has had time to take effect. But see how the losses due to the aircraft attack in the North Atlantic have declined. Here are the figures to the nearest thousand:

February	86,000	tons
March	69,000	"
April	59,000	"
May	21,000	"
June (to date)	18,000	"

Thus, this attack by aircraft, to which Hitler attached such importance and which seemed to be so loaded with menace, has not grown worse, but, on the contrary, at the present moment seems to have markedly dwindled away. The House should observe that the use of aircraft is not only defensive for our ships in convoy. It also tends to drive away the enemy aircraft and prevent them scouting for U-boats and guiding them to our ships. At the same time, our aircraft guide our own destroyers and corvettes to attack the U-boats themselves. Oppressed by these measures, the enemy has now been led to operate farther from our shores and he now ranges in the Western half of the Atlantic and in the South Atlantic. This drives him well into the zone in which the United States patrols are becoming increasingly effective. It also ruptures that deadly combination of the air and U-boat attack upon which Hitler had been encouraged by his advisers to build his hopes. Of course, I hope for very much greater aid from the United States, but this must come by itself, as I am sure it will do, in God's good time.

In the present phase we are much strained. The American

patrol does not as yet give us full security in the zones the President has certified, and the U-boat danger is so pronounced as to make it necessary for us to convoy right across the ocean. With our limited number of anti-U-boat vessels, this has meant halving the escorts, or something like it. But I hope this phase will pass. The rate of sinkings last winter led many people to doubt the value of the convoy system. Up to March, vessels over fifteen knots sailed independently, trusting to their speed and the size of the ocean spaces. The Admiralty, on whom in the last war the convoy system was forced, have now become its most strenuous advocates. We thought it right, however, to make the experiment of allowing ships which could steam thirteen knots or over, and then twelve knots or over, to sail independently. Experience seems to show that the convoy system is the best for anything except really fast ships, and in spite of the large convoys and the small escorts which our poverty forces upon us, it has now been decided to go back to the fifteen-knot limit below which nothing must sail independently. I should like the House to realize, however, that the whole question of convoy was not only re-examined but tested, and that both the Admiralty and the Ministry of Shipping, now merged in the Ministry of War Transport, are agreed about the fifteen-knot limit.

I shall have to recur in a few moments once again to the operational side, but I now turn to the position at the ports. At the beginning of March there were over 2,600,000 tons of damaged shipping accumulated in our ports, of which about 930,000 tons were ships undergoing repair while working cargo, and nearly 1,700,000 were immobilized by the need of repairs. The tonnage immobilized solely by repairs is the most injurious and obnoxious feature of the story. In my directive of March 6, which I read just now, I aimed at beating this down by 400,000 by July 1. But later on we became more ambitious, and we set ourselves as a target a reduction of 750,000 tons by the same date. We had a heavy blow as a result of the air attacks made on the Mersey and the Clyde at the beginning of May. These added many thousands of tons to the total of ship tonnage damaged at sea. We also had a windfall which added to the number of ships to be repaired. A number of ships given up as hopeless were rescued by our Salvage Service and added to the repair list. Nevertheless, in spite of these additions, unwelcome and welcome, the tonnage immobilized by reason of repair on June 12, the latest date for which I have figures, has been reduced to just under a million tons. This represents a gain, not yet indeed of the 750,000 tons at which we aimed, but of 700,000 tons, which is tolerably near it. Even although we remember, before we crow too much, that there is always a diminution in the summer weather of marine casualties, quite apart from enemy action, the figures I have mentioned should give rise not only to relief but to satisfaction.

Let us glance for a moment at some of the measures by which this result has been achieved. The first is, of course, the steady drive which is being made to increase the labor force on merchant-ship repairs. There are now in the private shipbuilding yards engaged on hull work, 11,000 more workers than at the end of January. There has also been a definite transfer from naval to merchant work. My right honorable friend the Minister of Labor has worked very hard at this.

Another economy in the turn-round has been effected by a simplification of degaussing. The brilliant and faithful servants who mastered the magnetic mine aspired naturally towards perfection in the degaussing system beyond what we can afford in these hard times. We have to balance risks against getting the ships quickly to sea. It is now very rare indeed for a ship to be delayed simply on account of degaussing repairs or improvements; either these are effected while the ship is discharging or loading or a certain amount of chance is taken. With Mr. Harriman's aid a proportion of the more thorough and more permanent installations is being effected in United States ports. There may well be a saving of two or three days in the turn-round on this process alone. Other savings have been effected by a more close concert of action between the naval and civil port authorities, and though I cannot put a precise figure on the total saving, it is certainly substantial and will be further increased. Never forget that the saving in the turn-round of a single day over the vast field of our traffic is worth a quarter of a million tons in effective imports during a year.

I have never allowed the excuse to be pleaded of congestion at our ports, because in spite of all our difficulties, we are in fact only handling and budgeting to handle about half the prewar traffic. Nonetheless, a great effort is being made. Inland sorting depots which enable the goods to be got away quickly from the air-raided quaysides into the country are commended by the Select Committee. Six of these are in process of construction to serve our west-coast ports. The first will come into partial operation in September. To get the best out of the South Wales ports we are quadrupling the railway line from Newport to the Severn Tunnel; part of the quadrupled line is already in operation. Some of the transport bottlenecks are found at inland junctions on the western side of the island because a greater strain is being cast upon them than they were constructed to bear. These are being opened up. A considerable development of overside discharge at suitable anchorages has been organized, not only as a relief but as an alternative in case of very heavy attack. A large expansion in our crane facilities is on foot, both to equip new emergency ports and to make existing port facilities more flexible under attack. In May alone, one hundred and thirty mobile cranes were delivered from British factories and from the United States as compared with the previous average of fifty in the last four months. I should trespass unduly upon the House if I were to describe this part of our struggle in any more detail.

I am now able to present some general conclusion. Our losses and those of our Allies by sinking in the last few months have been very heavy. In the last twelve months they amount to 4,600,000 tons. The enemy continually varies his form of attack in order to meet our countermeasures. We give him a hot time in the North Western Approaches, he opens up off the banks of Newfoundland or even nearer to the American coast. We deploy our escorts and our flying boats more widely, the United States Navy advances into the conflict, and the enemy develops heavy and effective U-boat attack off Dakar and in the Cape

Verde Islands area. Every move or new device on one side is met by a counter on the other.

It is because it is vital that the enemy should not know how much success attends these moves that we propose in the near future to stop the monthly publication of shipping losses. We have published the very heavy figures for May and also all the arrears which have come in later about the losses for April and March. The April and May figures were swollen by the severe fighting in the Mediterranean; it looks as if the June figures will be better, although, of course, at any moment a flock of U-boats getting into one of our convoys may upset our forecasts. At the present time, June 25, five days before the end of the month, we might hope to be within 300,000 tons. But then again there may be some arrears. Still, June in the middle of the summer will certainly show a better figure than February or March, those spring months in which Hitler boasted the fury of his attack would break upon us.

After June we do not propose to publish any more figures. It is giving too much help to the enemy to let him know each month the success or failure of his repeated variants of attack. He knows our figures are true; they are of the greatest value to him; I have no doubt the German Admiralty would pay £100,000 a month for the information we so meticulously compile and proclaim. We get nothing in return; he tells us nothing except extraordinary lies and exaggerations which have long since been discredited. Our task, our effort for survival, is surely hard enough without our becoming an effective branch of the German Intelligence Service. I have no doubt there will be a howl, not only from the Germans, but from some well-meaning patriots in this island. Let them howl. We have got to think of our sailors and merchant seamen, the lives of our countrymen, and of the life of our country, now quivering in the balance of mortal peril.

It would be a great mistake for us to ingeminate and emphasize our woes. I cannot share that sense of detachment which enables some people to feel they are rendering a public service by rubbing in the most dark and anxious part of our situation. Only the other day our great friend President Roosevelt stated some figures about our losses in relation to British and American new building in the most startling and alarming form. There was nothing very new about these figures and facts, and we gave our assent beforehand to the President's use of them. It certainly had a bad effect in all the balancing countries, in Spain, at Vichy, in Turkey, and in Japan.

The Japanese Ambassador, in taking leave the other day, a man most friendly to peace between our countries, inquired anxiously of me about Mr. Roosevelt's statement, which he evidently felt might be a factor in an adverse decision by Japan, which he hoped to avert. The House must not underrate the dangers of our plight. We cannot afford to give any advantages to the enemy in naval information, nor can we afford to paint our affairs in their darkest colors before the eyes of neutrals and to discourage our friends and encourage our foes all over the world.

I end upon this figure of 31,000,000 tons import in 1941, which I ask shall be kept most strictly secret. If we can bring this in, we can carry on our life at home and our war effort in the East without any further serious restrictions. If we fail to do it, we shall be definitely weakened in our struggle for existence and for the right to breathe the air of freedom. I believe we shall succeed, and it may even be there will be some improvement. This would become certain if we obtained more direct assistance from the flotillas and flying boats of the United States, and still more if the United States took the plunge in good time.

On the present showing, if we can resist or deter actual invasion this autumn, we ought to be able, on the present undertakings of the United States, to come through the year 1941. In 1942 we hope to be possessed of very definite air ascendancy, and to be able not only to carry our offensive bombing very heavily into Germany, but to redress to some extent the frightful strategic disadvantages we suffer from the present German control of the Atlantic seaports of Europe. If we can deny to the enemy or at least markedly neutralize the enemy-held Atlantic ports and airfields, there is no reason why the year 1942, in which the enormous American new building comes to hand, should not present us with less anxious ordeals than those we must now endure and come through.

I will add only one other word. Let us not forget that the enemy has difficulties of his own; that some of these difficulties are obvious; that there may be others which are more apparent to him than to us; and that all the great struggles of history have been won by superior will power wresting victory in the teeth of odds or upon the narrowest of margins.

THE WAR IN THE FAR EAST

ON WEDNESDAY, April 23, 1942, the House of Commons went into Secret Session to hear a long statement by Mr. Winston Churchill on the fall of Singapore and the war situation in the Far East. It was a somber, unhappy story of reverses on land, at sea, and in the air and the loss of many brave men, noble ships, and valuable armaments, but it ended with a further declaration of Mr. Churchill's unshakable confidence in final victory.

This speech, one of the longest and most revealing ever delivered by the Prime Minister during the war, was so fully and carefully prepared that it is possible to print here a complete and accurate record of what he almost certainly said.

He took Parliament completely into his confidence and did not attempt to minimize the grave reverses Britain and America had sustained in the Far East and elsewhere. He described how the Ark Royal, Barham, Prince of Wales, and Repulse had been sunk, and the battleships Nelson, Queen Elizabeth, and Valiant put out of action. He gave the startling news that in seven weeks a third of Britain's battleships and battle cruisers had been lost or crippled.

He revealed that when Singapore fell, a hundred thousand troops had surrendered to thirty thousand Japs. At the same time he rejected the idea of an investigation at that time of the Malaya disaster, as it would have hampered the prosecution of the war.

In his speech he surveyed the whole course and breadth of the conflict and he presented without reservation "the ugly realities" of the situation. He would not have dared to do this, he explained, if his confidence in the Allies' power to come through safe and victorious was in any way diminished.

THE FALL OF SINGAPORE

A speech to the

House of Commons

April 23, 1942

SINCE JAPAN became our enemy and the United States our Ally after December 7, the weight of the war upon us has become far more severe and we have sustained a painful series of misfortunes in the Far East. Apart from the stubborn and brave defense of the Bataan Peninsula by the United States, the brunt of the Japanese attacks has fallen almost entirely upon us and the Dutch. The United States fleet has not yet regained the command of the Pacific which was lost after Pearl Harbor: and while we are at war with Germany and Italy, we do not possess the naval resources necessary to maintain the command of the Indian Ocean against any heavy detachment from the main Japanese fleet. Before the Japanese entered the war, we were already fully extended in the North Sea, Atlantic, and Mediterranean theaters by sea, land, and air. We have drawn all possible forces to meet our new, fresh, and most formidable antagonist. But in spite of all we could do and the risks we ran and are running, we have been and are at present outnumbered by the sea, land, and air forces of Japan throughout the Far Eastern theater. This fact must be faced by all who wish to understand what has happened and what is going to happen.

From the beginning of our struggle with Hitler, I have always hoped for the entry of the United States; and although the ideal was to have America in while Japan remained out, I did not think that the injuries Japan would certainly inflict upon us in our ill-guarded and even denuded Eastern theater would be too heavy a price to pay for having the immense resources and power of the United States bound indissolubly to our side and to our cause. That is still my feeling. But I frankly admit that the violence, fury, skill, and might of Japan has far exceeded anything that we had been led to expect. The Japanese military performances in China had not seemed remarkable. The Chinese had always been a weak nation, divided, and traditionally unwarlike. We knew that they were very ill-armed and ill-supplied, especially with every weapon that matters in modern war. And yet for four and a half years the Japanese, using as many as a million men at a time, had failed to quell or conquer them. This seemed to give a line as to form. The event was different. Neither, of course, were we prepared for the temporary eclipse and paralysis of the United States sea power in the Pacific, which followed from the disaster at Pearl Harbor. The combination of these two factors has been very adverse to us.

Our military position at the outbreak of the Japanese war was as follows. I had obtained from President Roosevelt in October last shipping sufficient to carry two divisions additional to our ordinary heavy convoys from this country to the Middle East. The first of these divisions, the 18th, was rounding the Cape in the early days of December. It was destined for the Levant-Caspian front, which it then seemed so necessary to reinforce, and the 17th Indian Division was already preparing to move from India to this same theater, where the dangers of 1942 seemed mainly to lie. Both these divisions were immediately diverted to the Malay Peninsula. In the few days before I left for the United States we set in motion to India or Malaya other very considerable forces which we had on the water, including six antiaircraft and antitank units and two hundred and fifty aircraft. All these factors were sorely needed either in Libya, where General Auchinleck's offensive was at its height, or on the threatened Levant-Caspian front. The fact that they, and many other forces that have followed them, were turned to meet the new antagonist in no way lessens the need for them in the Middle East. This may become painfully apparent should the magnificent Russian defense of the approaches to the Caucasus be beaten down, or General Rommel be able to assume the offensive against Egypt in superior strength.

The House must face the position squarely. Not only have we failed to stem the advance of the new enemy, but we have had to weaken seriously the hopeful operations we were carrying on against the old. In all, in the first two months of the Japanese war, up to the time of the fall of Singapore, we had landed in the Malay Peninsula, or moved from India into Burma, 70,000 troops, 300 guns, a certain number of tanks, and 350 aircraft—all of which, I repeat, were taken away from actual fighting operations elsewhere. At the same time we began to move the Australian Army away from the Levant-Caspian front to sustain the Dutch in the East Indies or, as has since turned out, for a large number of them, to defend the homeland of Australia. The valiant and hitherto successful resistance of Russia has alone rendered these highly dangerous diversions possible without disastrous consequences so far. In spite of the results up to date, I remain convinced that the broad strategic dispositions which we made of our forces prior to the Japanese attack, and the redistributions made after that attack, were the best in our power. Sometimes, though not always, people are wise after the event, but it is also possible to be wise before the event and yet not have the power to stop it happening. In war misfortunes may come from faults or errors in the High Command. They may also come from the enemy being far too strong, or fighting far too well. It is easy when the tide is adverse to contend that alterations in the structure of the war direction would have made or will make amends for the vast and gaping lack of men and resources or power of transportation. It is easy, but it may not be true.

During these anxious times a series of unexampled losses fell upon the Royal Navy. On September 27 the *Nelson* had had her bows blown in by a torpedo and was put out of action for six months. On November 13 the *Ark Royal* was sunk in the Mediterrancan by a single torpedo—a feature most disquieting to our naval constructors. On November 25 the *Barham* foundered off Libya from a volley of torpedoes, with a loss of 800 men. Here again chance played a hard part.

The *Prince of Wales* and the *Repulse* arrived at Singapore on December 2. This seemed to be a timely moment. It was hoped that their presence there might be a deterrent upon the war party in Japan, and it was intended that they should vanish as soon as possible into the blue. I have already explained to the House how they became involved in a local operation against Japanese transports in the Gulf of Siam which led to their destruction. On the night of December 9, in view of the news we had received about the heavy losses of the American fleet at Pearl Harbor, I proposed to the Chiefs of the Staff that the *Prince of Wales* and *Repulse* should join the undamaged portion of the American fleet in order to sustain the position in the Pacific. The matter was to be further considered next day, but in the morning arrived the news of the loss of both these great ships. We had now no modern or modernized capital ships in the Indian Ocean. The remnants of the American Battle Fleet from Pearl Harbor were withdrawn a further two thousand miles or more to the Californian bases. Since then from San Francisco to Aden or Capetown, distances of about fourteen thousand miles, there has been no surface fleet capable of fighting a general action with the navy of Japan.

A further sinister stroke was to come. On the early morning of December 19 half a dozen Italians in unusual diving suits were captured floundering about in the harbor of Alexandria. Extreme precautions have been taken for some time past against the varieties of human torpedo or one-man submarine entering our harbors. Not only are nets and other obstructions used, but underwater charges are exploded at frequent irregular intervals in the fairway. Nonetheless, these men had penetrated the harbor. Four hours later explosions occurred in the bottoms of the *Valiant* and *Queen Elizabeth*, produced by limpet bombs fixed with extraordinary courage and ingenuity, the effect of which was to blow large holes in the bottoms of both ships and to flood several compartments, thus putting them both out of action for many months. One ship will soon be ready again, the other is still in the floating dock at Alexandria, a constant target for enemy air attack. Thus, we had no longer any battle squadron in the Mediterranean. *Barham* had gone, and now *Valiant* and *Queen Elizabeth* were completely out of action. Both these ships floated on an even keel, they looked all right from the air. The enemy were for some time unaware of the success of their attack, and it is only now that I feel it possible to make this disclosure to the House, even in the strictness of a Secret Session. The Italian fleet still contains four or five battleships, several times repaired, of the new *Littorio* or of the modernized class. According to prewar notions and indeed all paper calculations, there was no reason why a large German and Italian army should not have been ferried across to invade not merely Libya or Palestine or Syria, but Egypt itself. The sea defense of the Nile Valley had to be confided to our submarine and destroyer flotillas with a few cruisers and, of course, to shore-based air forces. For this reason it was necessary to transfer a part of our shore-based torpedo-carrying aircraft from the south and east coasts of England, where they were soon to be needed, to the North African shore. This movement was justifiable because of the absence of any preparation for immediate invasion apparent on the enemy's side of the Channel and because of his evident preoccupation with Russia. We may say these arrangements for the defense of Egypt have so far been successful. The very opportune and brilliant action by Admiral Vian when, favored by a happy slant of wind for his smoke screen, he made the Italian battleship turn tail in broad daylight by a mere attack of light cruisers and destroyers has been rightly applauded. It has, it will now be seen, a significance of a special character. We were, of course, left very bare in home waters. However, I have no doubt other resources will be at hand before the main German armies can again be transported to the west, and the invasion danger again become imminent.

These events and their sequence which I have mentioned to the House in Secret Session have a bearing upon the escape of the *Scharnhorst* and *Gneisenau* from their uncomfortable station at Brest. I have been impressed by the shock which the passage of these two ships through the Channel gave to the loyal masses of the British nation. Personally, with my special knowledge, I thought it a very annoying incident but not comparable at all to the other happenings I have just described. Our torpedo-carrying aircraft were depleted by the needs of Egypt. As to the Navy, we do not for obvious reasons keep capital ships in the narrow seas. Attention has, however, also been drawn to the fact that there were only six destroyers capable of attacking the German battle cruisers. Where, it is asked, were all the rest of our flotillas? The answer is that they were and are out on the approaches from the Atlantic, convoying the food and munitions from the United States without which we cannot live. However, there is a good plan which, should invasion again become imminent, will very rapidly multiply the flotillas in the narrow waters. The photographic reconnaissance of the enemy harbors, basins, and river mouths, made daily when the weather permits, should keep us well advised of any gathering of barges similar to that which took place in the summer and autumn of 1940. Moreover, in 1940 an invading force of perhaps 150,000 picked men might have created mortal havoc in our midst. But now our home army and Home Guard have grown and improved to such an extent that it would not be much use an invader coming with less than six or seven hundred thousand men and six or seven armored divisions with many thousands of vehicles. The enormous shipping movements and air activities which would be the indispensable prelude to this would certainly be detected. We therefore feel entitled to use the flotillas to the utmost on feeding the island and escorting the outward-bound troop and Russian convoys, and we also felt entitled to send to the African shore a considerable proportion of our coastal torpedo-carrying aircraft after the disappearance of our battle fleet in the Mediterranean. We hold ourselves answerable in the gravest manner to watch and handle judiciously this invasion danger, and I do not think you will ever have to run again the frightful hazards through which we passed in 1940.

I will digress for a moment from my general theme to comment further upon the passage of the *Scharnhorst* and *Gneisenau* up the Channel and through the Straits of Dover. Most people thought this very astonishing and very alarming. They could have broken south and perhaps got into the Mediterranean. They could have gone out into the Atlantic as commerce raiders. They could have gone north about and tried to reach their own home waters by the Norwegian fiords. But the one way which seemed impossible to the general public was that they could come up the Channel and through the Straits of Dover. I will therefore read an extract from the Admiralty appreciation which was written on the 2nd February, ten days before the cruisers broke out, and when their exercise and steam trials and arrival of escorting German destroyers showed what they had in mind:

At first sight this passage up the Channel appears hazardous for the Germans. It is probable, however, that, as their heavy ships are not fully efficient, they would prefer such passage, relying for their security on their destroyers and aircraft, which are efficient, and knowing full well that we have no heavy ships with which to oppose them in the Channel. We might well, therefore, find the two battle cruisers and the eight-inch cruiser with five large and five small destroyers, also, say, twenty fighters constantly overhead (with reinforcements within call), proceeding up Channel.

Taking all factors into consideration, it appears that the German ships can pass east up the Channel with much less risk than they will incur if they attempt an ocean passage to Norway, and as it is considered the Germans will evade danger until they are fully worked up, the Channel passage appears to be their most probable direction if and when they leave Brest.

I have read this document to the House because I am anxious that Members should realize that our affairs are not conducted entirely by simpletons and dunderheads as the comic papers try to depict, and in particular that the Admiralty, which I regard as an incomparable machine for British protection, in spite of all the misfortunes and accidents that have happened, deserves a very broad measure of confidence and gratitude. Considering their knowledge and foresight and the intense, indefatigable care which has brought us thus far safely on this hard voyage, I think they deserve to be regarded with respect. Any featherhead can have confidence in times of victory, but the test is to have faith when things are going wrong for the time being, and when things happen which cannot be explained in public.

I now return to my narrative and general argument. The House will see that in November and December last year in a few weeks we lost or had put out of action for a long time seven great ships or more than one-third of our battleships and battle cruisers, and that this happened at a time when we were fully extended and had to meet the attack of a new fresh and tremendous enemy and while our great Ally was temporarily entirely crippled at sea. It is upon this background and with this accompaniment that I will make a very few observations about the tragedy and disaster of Singapore.

On December 7, 1941, there were in Singapore and the Malay Peninsula about sixty thousand British, Australian, and Indian troops, and immediately after the declaration we set in motion to Malaya, as I have described, between forty and fifty thousand others, including a high proportion of technical arms. After a long rear-guard action down the Malay Peninsula, there were, according to the War Office figures, about one hundred thousand men gathered in the island of Singapore by the morning of February 3. On the night of February 8 about five thousand Japanese made a lodgment on the northwestern corner of the island and were gradually reinforced by landings from other points until perhaps thirty thousand men had been landed. After five or six days of confused but not very severe fighting, the army and fortress surrendered. The Japanese have not stated the number of prisoners they have taken, but it does not seem that there was very much bloodshed. This episode and all that led up to it seems to be out of harmony with anything that we have experienced or performed in the present war. Many explanatory factors are mentioned: the absence of the Air Force, owing to the enemy's domination of our airfields; the dispiriting effects of the long retreat upon the troops engaged in it; the enervating effects of the climate upon all Europeans; the fact that some of the reinforcements had been a long time on board ship; and, above all, the embarrassment to the defense caused by it being intermingled with a city containing at that time upwards of one million human beings of many races and conditions. In all these circumstances I do not at all wonder that requests should be made for an inquiry by a Royal Commission, not only into what took place upon the spot in the agony of Singapore but into all the arrangements which had been made beforehand. I am convinced, however, that this would not be good for our country, and that it would hamper the prosecution of the war. Australian accounts reflect upon the Indian troops. Other credible witnesses disparage the Australians. The lack of any effective counterattack by the 18th Division, which arrived in such high spirits and good order, and never seem to have had their chance, is criticized. The generalship is criticized. There is an endless field for recrimination. Most of those concerned are prisoners. General Wavell, who was in charge of the whole ABDA area from January 15 onwards, is far too busy grappling with new perils. We, too, have enough trouble on our hands to cope with the present and the future, and I could not in any circumstances consent to adding such a burden, for a heavy burden it would be, to those which we have to bear. I must ask the House to support the government in this decision, which is not taken in any ignoble desire to shield individuals or safeguard the administration, but solely in the interests of the state and for the successful prosecution of the war. The premature fall of Singapore led to failures of the resistance in Java and Sumatra. But this might have happened in any case in view of the decisive Japanese superiority in numbers and organization.

What has happened in Burma? About two divisions of Indian and Burmese troops, with a very few British battalions, have resisted and delayed the northward advance of powerful Japanese forces for over two months. West of the Sittang River they were reinforced by a brigade of tanks drawn from General Auchinleck's command, and by other British reinforcements. The remains of this force, which altogether had comprised perhaps the equivalent of three divisions, were driven back on Rangoon and were surrounded there. About this time, General Alexander arrived by air from England and infused new vigor into the wearied and outnumbered troops. Having very thoroughly destroyed the facilities of the city and harbor, he cut his way out to the north with his whole force and all their transport after hard fighting. Meanwhile a number of Chinese divisions had been slowly making their way southward and gradually came into line upon our eastern flank. These Chinese divisions are about as strong as British brigade groups, but they seem very capable of fighting the Japanese with constancy and courage.

A long, thin front was established diagonally facing southwards, and this front is being slowly driven north towards Mandalay and Lashio. The Japanese have been greatly aided by disloyal Burmese, and both Siamese and Burmese contingents are fighting with them. The British Imperial forces are astride the Irrawaddy and the main Rangoon-Burma road and railway. They are outnumbered by the Japanese who are being steadily reinforced from Rangoon, where at least one and possibly two fresh divisions have lately been landed.

General Wavell has been receiving in India all the aircraft we can transport and service, to the temporary detriment of General Auchinleck's operations in Libya. The United States are sending powerful air reinforcements, both in India and China. All this takes time, and the number of airfields at our disposal in Burma and the protection which it was possible to afford to them have not been sufficient to enable the British Air Force to maintain itself, and successive reinforcements have been wiped out, many of them on the ground as they arrived. General Wavell has also to consider the defense of northeastern India, which may at any time be gravely menaced. He is not therefore at present in a position to denude himself to any large extent, and he must not fritter away his resources. The difficulty is to get established on a sufficiently large scale and to maintain supplies and services in the test of Japanese superiority. Without this it is like throwing good money after bad, or throwing snowballs into a furnace to keep down the temperature. Efforts are being made to re-equip the American Volunteer Group working with the Chinese under the American general, General Stilwell, who has in every way shown himself a fine soldier and good comrade, and who has established the closest relations with General Alexander.

At the present time there is very little air support for our troops or for the Chinese, and Generalissimo Chiang Kai-shek has complained to me that he was promised air support which is not forthcoming when he ordered his divisions to march south into Burma. Mandalay and other towns have been the subjects of very severe air raids with great slaughter, and a huge flight of refugees is moving northward towards China, or westward in the hopes of reaching India over extremely primitive and half-constructed roads. Typhus and cholera have made their appearance behind our harassed front. Treachery and infiltration are rife. A tragic fate impends upon the mass of refugees collected to the north of Mandalay. In the midst of these scenes of indescribable misery and ruin, the Governor-General, whom we know so well in this House as Minister of Agriculture a couple of years ago, and his devoted wife have been a fountain of courage and inspiration.

The advance of the enemy has been greatly slowed down by the exertions of General Alexander and his American colleague and by the very brave fighting of the British, Indian, and Chinese troops still on the front. Our Imperial forces are however reduced to very small proportions. There is no means of bringing reinforcements to them by sea: the Japanese hold complete command of the Bay of Bengal, and only trickles of men and supplies can come over the mountain roads and tracks from Assam. General Wavell has the duty of distributing his resources to the best advantage, and we are sending him everything we can, having regard to our other responsibilities, which are neither few nor easy.

I cannot encourage the House to expect good news from the Burma theater. The best that can be hoped for is that the retreat will be as slow as possible and give time for other factors to make their weight tell.

At this point we may consider what Japanese strategy is likely to be. So far as we know, the Japanese have seventy-two field divisions with some additional brigades and a mass of trained soldiers which is certainly not less than two million additional behind them. Of these seventy-two divisions, twenty-seven are in the so-called ABDA area including Burma, fifteen are in China, twenty are opposite Russia in Manchuria, and only ten are left in Japan. The Japanese Army in the ABDA area threatens simultaneously Australia,

India, and, through Burma, China. They have conquered the whole of Malaya, the Philippines, and the Dutch East Indies. They have destroyed or captured the following divisions of the Allies or their equivalent. British and Indian, six; Dutch, three; United States, two; Filipinos, three or four. Total fourteen or fifteen. They may have lost a hundred thousand killed and wounded, but none of their divisional formations has been destroyed, and I make no doubt they can easily replace all casualties. They cost about a quarter to feed and carry of what British and still more American troops require. They certainly show no inferiority when they get to the spot. The Japanese armies, navy, and air force, working in close harmonious combination, being absolutely fresh after their many years of preparation and inculcation of war as the highest art and duty, having brought their plans up to date by fullest information and closest study of the German victories in Europe, and having added their own jungle craft thereto, have established themselves in little more than four months in the whole of these wide regions, which they call their Asiatic Co-Prosperity Sphere, from Luzon to Rangoon, and from the northern approaches of Australia to the southern approaches of China. In this vast area they have forces largely superior to any that we can bring to bear for a long time. They are no doubt sprawled and spread widely, but they are consolidating their positions to the full extent of their saved-up resources.

Which way will they go? Where will they strike next? Australia naturally fears immediate invasion, and the United States, which has accepted responsibility for everything east of a line drawn west of Australia, has sent and is sending continuous strong reinforcements. We have transported back to Australia a large part of the Australian Imperial forces from the Middle East. We do not see here that the Japanese would get great advantages by invading Australia in force. By so doing they would commit themselves to a very formidable campaign, at a great distance from home, with American sea power, as it regains its strength, operative on their communications. No doubt the Japanese will do their utmost to threaten and alarm Australia and to establish lodgments and bases on the northern part of Australia in order to procure the greatest locking up of Allied forces in that continent. We have done and will continue to do everything in our power to sustain our kith and kin. I have also procured from President Roosevelt a substantial reinforcement of United States troops for New Zealand, whose attitude and morale have been admirable. But neither Great Britain nor the United States must be drawn into immobilizing in Australasia undue numbers of the limited forces which they can transport across the sea within any given period.

Alternatively, the Japanese may invade India. There is no doubt of their ability, if they chose to concentrate their efforts, to invade and overrun a large part of India, to take Calcutta and Madras, and certainly to make very cruel air raids upon defenseless Indian cities.

The Japanese have not told us what they intend to do, so I can only make a guess, which I do under all reserves, knowing well the fallibility of human foresight in the fog of war. It would seem, however, looking at it from their point of view, that their best plan would be to push right ahead northwards from Burma into China, and try to finish up Chinese resistance and the great Chinese leader, Generalissimo Chiang Kai-shek. We have not noticed any Japanese movement lately which is inconsistent with this idea, but there are several which support it. Certainly by driving China out of the war and possibly installing another puppet government in China, which would be their ally, Japan would seem to be greatly furthering her own interests. China is the only place where Japan can obtain a major decision in her favor in 1942. Moreover, let me point out, this process, if successful, would be to Japan one of contraction and not of further perhaps excessive expansion. It would be entirely in harmony with a Japanese attack on Russia, for which many preparations have been made. It would certainly release a good many Japanese divisions for further enterprise in a subsequent year. Of course, this appreciation may be wrong, but it is what seems most in the interests of the enemy and therefore most to be feared.

Before I leave the Far Eastern theater with its dark panorama of ruin, actual, and prospective, I will deal with the naval situation and the air situation as it affects naval operations in the Indian Ocean and the Bay of Bengal.

The surprise of Pearl Harbor threw the American Pacific Fleet, on which so much depended, out of action for the time being; and though the losses have been largely made good, the American fleet has remained separated from the enemy by the vast distances of the Pacific, and has been mainly concerned with maintaining communications with Australia, along which considerable forces are passing. The

Japanese Navy lies in the center of the scene, and like the Japanese Army it can strike in either direction. Our Eastern Fleet in the Indian Ocean cannot tell with any certainty what size or strength of Japanese vessels will emerge from the Malay Archipelago, through the Straits of Malacca or the Straits of Sunda. We cannot tell how far the Japanese preoccupations about the American Navy will force them to retain the bulk of their naval power in their home waters or in the Eastern Pacific. We do not know whether the Japanese wish to fight a battle with any American naval forces which may be operating in the islands between the American continent and Australia. Obviously, if the main part of the Japanese Navy comes west into the Indian Ocean we, with our other tasks on hand, would not be able to fight the fleet action. On the other hand, when and in proportion as they get tied to the American sphere by the reviving strength of the American Navy, our control of the Indian Ocean will improve, provided of course we are not brought to action and defeated in the meantime. The fact, however, that the Japanese have at present a move either way, and can undoubtedly move our way in largely superior strength, confronts the Admiralty and the Commander-in-Chief of our Eastern Fleet with most vexatious and difficult problems, not capable perhaps for some months of a satisfactory solution.

After virtual annihilation of British, Dutch, and United States light forces in Javanese waters and the loss of Singapore, Java, and Sumatra, we naturally considered Ceylon as a key point we have to hold. This cannot be done without adequate shore-based aircraft and ample antiaircraft artillery.

Our resources were limited and there are, as I have said, many clamant calls upon them. However, casting aside a great many other needs, we did manage to give a considerable measure of protection to Colombo and Trincomalee, and also to place in Ceylon military forces sufficient to require a substantial invading army to overcome them. All through March we were most anxious about Ceylon because of our weak condition there. But by the end of March we began to feel a little more comfortable; and this feeling persists so far.

In the last days of March, Admiral Somerville, who commands our Eastern Fleet, and who, as I said, is fresh from two years of almost continuous fighting in the Mediterranean and has conducted at least twenty extremely tricky and hazardous operations there—who is perhaps more familiar than any other man except Admiral Cunningham with the conditions of modern air attack on ships of war, who has run many convoys into Malta, raided Genoa, and taken part in all kinds of actions—formed the impression, from what scraps of information he could pick up, that a Japanese incursion into the Bay of Bengal was probable. It was also thought that there might well be a certain number of aircraft carriers supported by three Kongo battle cruisers. These are old battle cruisers modernized like every other large ship in the Japanese Navy (we, of course, only modernized a few of ours) and they carry fourteen-inch guns.

I am not, of course, going to tell what our naval strength was, is, or will be in these waters, but I will go as far as to say that we should have been happy to fight an action with a force of this kind. Accordingly, Admiral Somerville took station southeast of Ceylon, where he would be most likely to encounter the enemy, and our Catalina aircraft, which were on the spot, made far-ranging reconnaissances. There was no sign of the enemy and it became necessary for the fleet to go back to refuel. The Admiral came to the conclusion that the intelligence which had led him to expect the Japanese naval advance into the Indian Ocean was faulty. The whole work of the Navy has to be carried on. One of his two eight-inch gun cruisers, the *Cornwall*, was needed for an Australian troop convoy, and the other had to undergo certain necessary repairs. He sent both to Colombo. The *Hermes*, one of our oldest aircraft carriers, also had a mission to perform, and had to pick up various essentials at Trincomalee. No sooner had the Admiral dispersed his concentration than what he had formerly expected came to pass. A report was received of a large Japanese fleet steering northwestward towards Ceylon. The reconnaissance Catalina aircraft was shot down before it could describe exactly the composition of the enemy fleet. Immediately Admiral Somerville, who had by now completed refueling, issued orders to concentrate his ships. He expected to meet the three Kongos and perhaps two aircraft carriers together with ancillaries, and though he saw he could not intercept them before they attacked Colombo, he hoped to bring them to action should they tarry or should any of them be crippled by the counterattack of our shore-based bombers. He therefore fixed a rendezvous for his forces, told the *Dorsetshire* and *Cornwall* to get out of Colombo harbor and join him at this sea point, and he told *Hermes* at Trincomalee to go to sea and keep out of the way. The Admiralty did not interfere at all in these dispositions. When they put one of their best admirals in charge of a fleet and a theater, they do not stand over him with a stick, jogging his elbow. It is only very rarely when they possess exceptional knowledge that they override the judgment of the man on the spot. If the Admiralty does too much of that they simply destroy the whole initiative and responsibility of the admirals at sea. Such a bad habit, only acquired through wireless telegraphy, would be entirely contrary to the traditions of the Royal Navy. But, of course, if the House thinks fit, it may blame me for whatever went wrong.

At daylight on April 5 the Japanese Air Force attacked Colombo. All was in readiness for them. The harbor was largely cleared of ships; the *Cornwall* and *Dorsetshire* were, as Admiral Somerville thought, safe at sea; the antiair-raid precautions worked well; our fighters were in the air; and the enemy was beaten off with the loss of probably two-thirds of the aircraft they used in the attack. The counterattack by our Blenheims upon the enemy's aircraft carriers returned without finding them, but later in the day a Japanese reconnaissance plane sighted the *Cornwall* and *Dorsetshire* on their way to join Admiral Somerville's fleet. Both these ships were sunk in about a quarter of an hour by attacks of from forty to sixty fighter aircraft carrying one single large bomb each. Three-quarters of the ships' crews were, however, saved.

Here is another example of the formidable quality of the Japanese seaborne Air Force. Our cruisers have on many occasions in the Mediterranean been exposed to prolonged attacks by German and Italian aircraft and, though often damaged, have rarely been sunk, and in two cases only have they been sunk without all their antiaircraft ammunition having been used up. The fact that the Japanese, in spite of their heavy losses in the morning, could provide so large a force to attack the cruisers made it clear that they were employing a greater number of aircraft carriers than had been expected. In fact, there were found to be no fewer than five. In these circumstances it would have been wrong to force a fleet action, and Admiral Somerville, with the full approval of the Admiralty, withdrew into the wastes of the Indian Ocean.

The way was now open for any Japanese seaborne invasion of Ceylon. However, this did not take place. Instead the Japanese raided Trincomalee, where they were again severely rebuffed. They caught the *Hermes*, which had been ordered to clear out of the harbor, and inflicted very heavy losses, nearly one hundred thousand tons, upon our shipping in the Bay of Bengal.

It seems now that the enemy has retired to replenish his aircraft carriers after their heavy losses, and that his incursion into the Bay of Bengal was a foray and demonstration with an intention to bring off a Pearl Harbor surprise at Colombo.

I am not able to tell the House what we are doing in this lull. I can speak of the past, but not even in Secret Session of the present and future, but it ought not to be assumed that we are doing nothing. On the contrary, we have every hope that we shall presently be stronger in the Indian Ocean than hitherto. The unpleasant fact remains that for the present the enemy has effective command of the Bay of Bengal. Ceylon is the objective which would be most valuable to him, and it is there that we are most prepared.

I now leave the lesser war—for such I must regard this fearful struggle against the Japanese—and come to the major war against Germany and Italy. I will begin with the gravest matter, namely, the enormous losses and destruction of shipping by German U-boats off the east coast of the United States. In a period of less than sixty days, more tonnage was sunk in this one stretch than we had lost all over the world during the last five months of the Battle of the Atlantic before America entered the war. Most of all has this loss been heavy in tankers; indeed, the loss has been so severe that we have for some time past been withdrawing our own ships from the route. Our oil reserves are happily large, though the utmost economy must be practiced. We have done our best to aid the Americans in establishing a convoy system, and this will soon be brought into being. At their request, to assist the Americans we have sent over a number of our officers most experienced in anti-U-boat warfare, and upwards of thirty corvettes and antisubmarine craft from our own hard-pressed store. The figures for the last two months on the American coast, plus those in the Indian and Pacific Oceans from the Japanese attacks, constitute totals of monthly losses which are most alarming and formidable and comparable to the worst I have witnessed either in the last war or in this. On the other side, it must be remembered that the United States brought into the pool of Allied shipping upwards of nine million gross tons, so that the tonnage at the disposal of the Allies today is substantially greater than at this time last year, though at the same time the calls on our fleets are also increased. Moreover, I feel confident that the countermeasures which are being taken will be successful as they have been in the Battle of the Atlantic, and that the sinkings will presently be reduced to manageable proportions. I must, however, repeat that tonnage sinkings and the multiplication of U-boats constitute my greatest anxiety. It is only by the expansion of tonnage over losses, which will occur when the shipbuilding power of the United States makes itself felt, that easement will be given on the oceans which separate the United States from the rest of the world and the strength of the great Republic be enabled to come increasingly into action.

It is only by shipping that the United States or indeed ourselves can intervene, either in the Eastern or the Western theater. People speak airily of moving armies hither and thither. They do not know how harsh is the tonnage stringency, especially for ships of a suitable speed to carry troops, and how rigorous are the limitations which time and numbers impose upon our actions. Nevertheless, since the new war started we have actually moved from this country or from the Middle East across the sea against Japan more than 300,000 men, and we have over a hundred thousand on salt water at the present time. All these great convoys have hitherto been carried through the perils of mines and U-boat attacks without any appreciable loss of any kind since the beginning of the war. I regard this as a prodigy of skill and organization on the part of all those responsible for it.

I now come to the Middle East. Our strongest and best-equipped army overseas stands in close contact with the enemy in Cyrenaica. Twice have we hunted the enemy out of the Benghazi triangle and twice have we been chased back ourselves. The very severe battle which General Auchinleck fought last year just missed being a decisive victory. By what narrow margins, chances, and accidents was the balance tipped against us no one can compute. When I last spoke on this subject I said: "If not a victory, it was a highly profitable transaction." That is true. We inflicted three times the loss on the enemy that we suffered ourselves. We have fifty per cent more prisoners in our hands than we lost from all causes. Tobruk, after its stubborn defense, was relieved and is now a valuable supply base. The Gazala position, strongly fortified and strongly held, is one hundred and fifteen miles west of the starting point of our advance and two hundred and forty miles from our old lines at Mersa Matruh. Sollum Halfaya Pass and all that are in our hands. Our advancing railway runs through Fort Capuzzo and approaches El Adem. We maintain and maneuver considerable forces in this region. It is no use speculating what General Auchinleck or the enemy will try to do. Both sides have repaired their strength after the battle and the numbers which might engage are considerably larger than before.

But the fact that we do not possess Benghazi has a serious bearing upon the defense of Malta, because we cannot give continuous daylight air protection to our convoys to Malta from Egypt. For now nearly two years Malta has stood against the enemy. What a thorn it has been in their side! What toll it has taken of their convoys! Can we wonder that a most strenuous effort has been made by Germany and Italy to rid themselves of this fierce, aggressive foe. For the last six weeks over four hundred and fifty German first-line strength in aircraft and perhaps two hundred Italian have been venting their fury on Malta. An unending, intermittent bombardment has fallen upon the harbor and city, and sometimes as many as three hundred aircraft have attacked in a single day. The terrific ordeal has been borne with exemplary fortitude by the garrison and people. Very heavy losses have been inflicted upon the enemy's air strength. Malta is the first instance of an air force being maintained at odds often of ten to one from so few airfields all under constant bombardment. We replenish Malta with aircraft by all means in our power. The President has helped us with one of his best aircraft carriers, which has just completed a successful operation. We are stronger now than we have been, but the struggle is very hard and the question of supply and replenishment dangerous, difficult, and costly. The supply of food and ammunition is our constant care and our increasing anxiety.

If you add the air forces facing us in the Mediterranean to those which face us across the Channel and the North Sea, or are detained in Germany to meet our bomber offensive, we account for two-thirds of the German fighter strength and more than one-third of their bomber strength. We are also detaining in the Mediterranean area more than a thousand Italian first-line aircraft. Evidently this is a solid help to Russia. Both across the Channel and in the Malta fighting we have this year inflicted considerably heavier losses of aircraft than we have ourselves sustained. It is our interest to engage the enemy's air power at as many points as possible to make him bleed and burn and waste on the widest fronts and at the utmost intensity, and it pays us to lose machine for machine. We have done much better than that.

Therefore, every day that the air battle for Malta continues, grievous as it is to the island, its defenders and its gallant inhabitants, it plays its part in our general war effort and in helping our Russian allies. It may be that presently the German Air Forces attacking Malta will have to move eastward to sustain the impending offensive against southern Russia. If so, we shall have topped the ridge. Meanwhile the struggle at Malta is very hard. It is too early to say how it will end. But all the time we watch with admiration and with gratitude this protracted, undaunted, heroic conflict.

No one will accuse me of glozing over with a smooth and thin veneer the ugly realities of our situation. On the contrary, I thought the House would wish to have its darkest features underlined. But I would not have dared to do this if my confidence in our power to come through safe and victorious was in any way diminished, and I will now proceed to that part of my argument which will give reasons for this. If we are anxious about the sea, our enemies must be more anxious about the air. The gigantic American shipbuilding program, with our own comparatively modest contribution of twelve hundred thousand tons a year, will in 1943 give a very large favorable balance over sinkings, calculated even at a rate of half a million tons a month. We shall be very tight this year, but we ought to be a good deal better off next year. On the other hand, the Axis air power, upon which the enemy has so largely relied and by which so many of his triumphs have been gained, is certainly falling behind in the race. The recent estimates of American aircraft production, which seemed so extravagant, have so far been not only made good but exceeded. It is calculated that by July, 1942, the American, British, and Russian production of aircraft will be nearly three times that of Germany, Italy, and Japan. Now, of course, it takes some months for an impulsion of this character to be felt upon the fighting fronts. Transportation rears her ugly head. But it is only a matter of six or nine months before a marked preponderance of air power should manifest itself upon our side. At present there are more pilots than aircraft, but we have in no way slackened off our training of pilots. On the contrary, we are stimulating it because quite soon—in fact, during this autumn, we hope—the flood of aircraft will overtake and bear forward on its crest the very great numbers of pilots who are being trained.

In particular, the air position of Japan deserves scrutiny. According to our information, the Japanese losses and wastage greatly exceed and perhaps are nearly double their output, and the Japanese are separated by vast distances from any assistance by their confederates. One cannot tell where the various fronts of the Japanese war will be stabilized. But that we and the United States will presently be very much stronger in the air on all those fronts may be soberly but confidently expected. As this process goes on it will make a great deal of difference to the war in the whole Asiatic theater. What has been lost wholesale may be regained bit by bit, and after that perhaps more quickly. Our hope is that it will not be long before we have a fleet in the Indian Ocean well supported by seaborne and shore-based aircraft, which will be sufficiently powerful to challenge any major detachment of the Japanese Navy. At the same time the United States fleet in the Pacific will gain very large accessions of strength and, apart from the hazards of war, which we must never forget, will become even before the end of this year markedly superior to the whole Japanese Navy. The islands and bases which the Japanese have lightly acquired will become very heavy hostages to fortune. All this is carefully weighed and calculated out and various important enterprises are afoot. The aircraft carriers which are being built or rapidly adapted are numbered not by dozens but by scores, and it may well be that even before the end of this summer Japanese cities will begin to feel the weight of an air attack of which they on Sunday morning received only a foretaste—and squealed well. On no account let any word be spoken in disparagement of the war effort and war impulse of the United States. Our lives depend upon the growing application of their power.

Thus we may look to a fairly rapid acquisition of general air superiority, to a solid re-establishment of sea power both in the Indian and Pacific Oceans and, though this has to be toiled for, to the expansion in spite of losses of our transportation by sea.

But it is in Europe that the immediate main clash impends. Everything goes to show that perhaps even before the end of May Hitler will hurl a renewed offensive upon Russia, and there are no indications which contradict the general impression that his main thrust will be towards the Caspian and the Caucasus. We do not know what reserves the Russians have gathered. Everybody has always underrated the Russians. They keep their own secrets alike from foe and friends. The renewed German onslaught will start this year perhaps somewhat earlier and certainly a good deal farther east than last year. But this time there will be no surprise on the Russian side. Terrible injuries have been inflicted during the winter by the Russian armies, not only upon the German military power, but biting and searing deep into the whole life of the Nazi regime. With all its power and organization, it is a haggard Germany that Hitler leads into this new, ferocious, and sanguinary campaign, against Russia. Behind lies a Europe writhing with hatred and thirsting for revolt.

What can we do to help Russia? There is nothing that we would not do. If the sacrifice of thousands of British lives would turn the scale, our fellow countrymen would not flinch. But at this present time there are two important contributions we can make. The first is the supply of munitions to the utmost extent which our shipping can carry. We have hitherto not failed in any way in the immense undertakings which we made to Stalin. It is not, however, only a question of giving up what we need ourselves, but of carrying it there safely and punctually. Our northern convoys are a task of enormous difficulty and hazard. For the next few weeks the ice drifts lower and lower, and the channel between the ice floes and the North Cape becomes narrower. We convoy not only our own contribution but that of the United States, which to a large extent is taken from what the United States would otherwise have given us. Our ships and their escorts, the heaviest we have ever used, are pressed by the ice ever nearer to the shores of Norway, and large numbers of German U-boats and powerful air forces can strike continually at the merchant ships and their guardians.

There is a further serious complication—the *Tirpitz,* the *Scheer* and the *Hipper* lie in Trondheim fiord. Every British-American convoy to Russia is liable to attack by swift, heavy, modern German surface ships. Battleship escort has to be provided on every occasion. The enemy has great opportunities, by threatening attack upon the convoys and laying traps of U-boats, of inflicting vital losses upon our fleet. Serious risks are run by our great ships—so few, so precious—only one where in the last war there was a squadron of eight—every time they go north on this perilous duty; at any time the Admiralty or even the Minister of Defense may have to account to you for some loss which would take five years to replace. I cannot speak of our naval dispositions further than to say that the United States are with us on this. It is a grim and bitter effort amid fearful gales and ceaseless perils, but if it be in human power we will carry our tanks, our aircraft, and all the other essential supplies to our heroic ally in his sublime struggle.

There is another immediate way in which we can help. While the German armies will be bleeding copiously upon a two-thousand-mile front in the East we shall be on their backs in the German homeland. The British bombing offensive upon Germany has begun. Half a dozen German cities have already received the full measure that they meted out to Coventry. Another thirty or more are on the list. We have improved methods of finding the targets and built-up areas by night. The wastage of bombs has been reduced, perhaps by half. Daylight thrusts far into the heart of Germany, striking with deadly precision at the most sensitive industrial spots—such as the immortal feat of arms on Friday last—will be launched upon the enemy. Presently—indeed, quite soon—heavy United States formations will be established here in England and will work at our side. This summer and autumn—aye, and winter, too—Germany will experience scientific and accurate bombing of a weight and upon a scale and frequency which none of the nations they have maltreated has ever endured. We must not let false guides divert our minds from these major and terrible strokes of war, or tempt us to fritter away the solid mass of our endeavor. I heard a pretended British voice on the German radio the other night which said:

> We should know better than anyone that the "bombardment" of towns can't bring the end of the war nearer. London withstood about as heavy a bombardment as could be launched —something compared with which the raid on Tokyo can't have been more than a pinprick. The proper use of aircraft is to support land forces in the actual battle zone, and as the RAF isn't large enough to fulfill all its tasks, it should be reserved for this purpose only. A daylight raid on Augsburg, for instance, may be spectacular, but its practical value is negligible. They say we had six hundred planes up yesterday. It's a pity they weren't up over Burma, defending our stricken forces there.

Plausible—but is it disinterested?

All this leads me to the final point I have to make. When I went to the United States in December last I proposed to the President the preparation of a combined British and American invasion of German-occupied Europe for the liberation of its enslaved peoples and for the ultimate destruction of Hitlerism.

The war cannot be ended by driving Japan back to her

own bounds and defeating her overseas forces. The war can only be ended through the defeat in Europe of the German armies, or through internal convulsions in Germany produced by the unfavorable course of the war, economic privations, and the Allied bombing offensive. As the strength of the United States, Great Britain, and Russia develops and begins to be realized by the Germans, an internal collapse is always possible, but we must not count upon this. Our plans must proceed upon the assumption that the resistance of the German Army and Air Force will continue at its present level and that their U-boat warfare will be conducted by increasingly numerous flotillas.

We have, therefore, to prepare for the liberation of the captive countries of western and southern Europe by the landing at suitable points, successively or simultaneously, of British and American armies strong enough to enable the conquered populations to revolt. By themselves they will never be able to revolt, owing to the ruthless countermeasures that will be employed: but if adequate and suitably equipped forces were landed in several of the following countries, namely, Norway, Denmark, Holland, Belgium, and the French Channel coasts and the French Atlantic coasts, as well as Italy and possibly the Balkans, the German garrisons would prove insufficient to cope both with the strength of the liberating forces and the fury of the revolting peoples. It is impossible for the Germans, while we retain the sea power necessary to choose the place or places of attack, to have sufficient troops in each of these countries for effective resistance. In particular, they cannot move their armor about laterally from north to south or west to east:

either they must divide it between the various conquered countries—in which case it would become hopelessly dispersed—or they must hold it back in a central position in Germany, in which case it will not arrive until large and important lodgments have been made by us from overseas.

We had expected to find United States attention concentrated upon the war with Japan, and we prepared ourselves to argue that the defeat of Japan would not spell the defeat of Hitler, but that the defeat of Hitler left the finishing off of Japan merely a matter of time and trouble. We were relieved to find that these simple but classical conceptions of war, although vehemently opposed by the powerful isolationist faction, were earnestly and spontaneously shared by the government and dominant forces in the United States. The visit of General Marshall and Mr. Hopkins was to concert with us the largest and the swiftest measures of this offensive character. It will no doubt become common knowledge that the liberation of the Continent by equal numbers of British and American troops is the main war plan of our two nations. The timing, the scale, the method, the direction of this supreme undertaking must remain unknown and unknowable till the hour strikes and the blows fall. More than that I cannot say—except that in the early hours of this morning I received a message from the President of which, since we are in Secret Session, I will read the material part:

> I am delighted with the agreement which was reached between you and your military advisers and Marshall and Hopkins. They have reported to me of the unanimity of opinion relative

to the proposal which they carried with them and I appreciate ever so much your personal message confirming this.

I believe that this move will be very disheartening to Hitler and may well be the wedge by which his downfall will be accomplished. I am very heartened at the prospect and you can be sure that our army will approach the matter with great enthusiasm and vigor.

While our mutual difficulties are many, I am frank to say that I feel better about the war than at any time in the past two years.

Testing, trying, adverse, painful times lie ahead of us. We must all strive to do our duty to the utmost of our strength. As the war rises remorselessly to its climax, the House of Commons, which is the foundation of the British life struggle—this House of Commons which has especial responsibilities—will have the opportunity once again of proving to the world that the firmness of spirit, sense of proportion, steadfastness of purpose which have gained it renown in former days, will now once again carry great peoples and a greater cause to a victorious deliverance.

THE NORTH AFRICAN EXPEDITION

When the Anglo-American landings in North Africa were successfully carried out in December, 1942, there was some concern, both in Britain and America, at the acceptance of Admiral Darlan as the French leader and the Allied co-operation with him.

In a speech at a Secret Session of the House of Commons on December 10, 1942, Mr. Winston Churchill told the full story of the expedition and the reasons for the dealings with Darlan, who was assassinated a few weeks later.

In accordance with his practice when making statements of major importance, Mr. Churchill carefully prepared the full text of his speech. He made it clear that the decision to recognize Darlan as the French leader in North Africa was made by General Eisenhower and endorsed by President Roosevelt; and that personally he agreed with it.

Mr. Churchill also read messages between himself and the President about Darlan and emphasized that military expediency was the only consideration.

DARLAN AND THE NORTH AFRICAN LANDINGS

A speech to the
House of Commons
December 10, 1942

I HAVE first of all an announcement to make about the unshackling of prisoners. Last week the Germans officially informed the International Red Cross that they intended to unshackle all prisoners for the Christmas week. We had previously suggested to the protecting power that they should ask both countries to unshackle and we had told them that we would immediately comply with such a request. The protecting power has now made the request and instructions have been given by us to unshackle the German prisoners in our hands on December 12. I do not know what the response of the Germans to the protecting power will be, but in view of their statement about unshackling for Christmas there certainly seems a good chance that they will relieve our officers and men from the indignities they so wrongfully inflicted upon them. At any rate, that is what we are going to do.

I should like to make it clear that we have never had any object but to get our men unchained and it remains to be seen whether we shall achieve that object or not. There has never been in our minds any thought of reprisals in the sense of inflicting cruelty for cruelty's sake. On the other hand, it does not do to give way to a bully like Hitler. I am aware that many good people have criticized the action we took, but it may be that that action and the timing of its cessation will produce the result we aimed at, namely, the relief of our men. If so, it will be a matter for general satisfaction. In order that the Swiss action may have the best chance of success, the House will realize the importance of discretion in public discussion during the next few days.

I now come to certain aspects of the considerable enterprise which we and the United States have launched in French Northwest Africa, to which for convenience some months ago I gave the code name of TORCH.

On August 26, on my return from Moscow I telegraphed as follows to President Roosevelt:

"As I see this operation, it is primarily political in its foundations. The first victory we have to win is to avoid a battle. The second, if we cannot avoid it, to win it. In order to give us the best chances of the first victory we must (a) present the maximum appearance of overwhelming strength at the moment of the first attack, and (*b*) attack at as many places as possible. This is an absolutely different kind of operation from the Dieppe business. There we were up against German efficiency and the steel-bound, fortified coasts of France. In TORCH we have to face, at the worst, weak, divided opposition and an enormous choice of striking points at which to land. Risks and difficulties will be doubled by delay and will far outstrip increase of our forces. Careful planning in every detail, safety first in every calculation, far-seeing provisions for a long-term campaign, to meet every conceivable adverse contingency, however admirable in theory, will ruin the enterprise in fact.

"In order to lighten the burden of responsibility on the military commanders, I am of opinion that you and I should lay down the political data and take the risk upon ourselves. In my view, it would be reasonable to assume (*a*) that Spain will not go to war with Britain and the United States on account of TORCH; (*b*) that it will be at least two months before the Germans can force their way through Spain or procure some accommodation from her; (*c*) that the French resistance in North Africa will be largely token resistance, capable of being overcome by the suddenness and scale of the attack, and that thereafter the North African French may actively help us under their own Commanders; (*d*) that Vichy will not declare war on the United States and Great Britain; (*e*) that Hitler will put extreme pressure on Vichy, but that in October he will not have the forces available to overrun unoccupied France while at the same time we keep him pinned in the Pas de Calais, etc."

The last of these forecasts was falsified because the

French never made any resistance to the overrunning of the Unoccupied Zone, but all the others have so far been borne out by events. I quote them to show how much politics, apart from strategy, were involved in our joint plan, and how we hoped to reduce bloodshed and risk of failure to a minimum by utilizing the help of Frenchmen who were then in the service of the Vichy government. Into this scheme of things there swam quite unexpectedly, as I shall presently relate, the very important figure of Admiral Darlan.

I do not at all wonder that this Darlan business has caused a good deal of concern in this country, and I am glad to give an explanation of it. The question, however, which we must ask ourselves is not whether we like or do not like what is going on, but what are we going to do about it. In war it is not always possible to have everything go exactly as one likes. In working with allies it sometimes happens that they develop opinions of their own. Since 1776 we have not been in the position of being able to decide the policy of the United States. This is an American expedition in which they will ultimately have perhaps two or three times as large ground forces as we have, and three times the air force. On sea the proportion is overwhelmingly in our favor, and we have, of course, given a vast amount of organization and assistance in every way. Nevertheless, the United States regards this as an American expedition under the ultimate command of the President of the United States, and they regard Northwest Africa as a war sphere which is in their keeping, just as we regard the eastern Mediterranean as a theater for which we are responsible. We have accepted this position from the outset and are serving under their command. That does not mean we have not got a great power of representation, and I am, of course, in the closest touch with the President. It does mean, however, that neither militarily nor politically are we directly controlling the course of events. It is because it would be highly detrimental to have a debate upon American policy or Anglo-American relations in public that His Majesty's government have invited the House to come into Secret Session. In Secret Session alone can the matter be discussed without the risk of giving offense to our great Ally and also of complicating the relationships of Frenchmen, who, whatever their past, are now firing upon the Germans.

I hold no brief for Admiral Darlan. Like myself he is the object of the animosities of Herr Hitler and of Monsieur Laval. Otherwise I have nothing in common with him. But it is necessary for the House to realize that the government and to a large extent the people of the United States do not feel the same way about Darlan as we do. He has not betrayed *them*. He has not broken any treaty with them. He has not vilified them. He has not maltreated any of their citizens. They do not think much of him, but they do not hate him and despise him as we do over here. Many of them think more of the lives of their own soldiers than they do about the past records of French political figures. Moreover, the Americans have cultivated up to the last moment relations with Vichy, which were of a fairly intimate character and which in my opinion have conduced to our general advantage. At any rate, the position of the Americans at Vichy gave us a window on that courtyard which otherwise would not have existed.

Admiral Leahy has been Ambassador to Vichy until quite recently. He lived on terms of close intimacy with Marshal Pétain. He has at all times used his influence to prevent Vichy France becoming the ally of Germany or declaring war upon us when we have had to fire on Vichy troops at Oran or Dakar, in Syria or in Madagascar. On all these occasions I have believed, and have recorded my opinion beforehand, that France would not declare war; but a factor in forming that opinion was the immense American influence upon all Frenchmen, which influence, of course, increased enormously after the United States entered the war. Admiral Leahy is a close friend of President Roosevelt and was recently appointed his personal Chief of the Staff. The attitude of the United States executive and State Department towards Vichy and all its works must be viewed against this background.

Since we broke with Vichy in 1940, this country has had no contacts with French North Africa, or only very slender and hazardous secret contacts. The Americans, on the other hand, have roamed about Morocco, Algiers, and Tunisia without the slightest impediment, with plenty of money and with a policy of trade favors to bestow. They have worked all this time, both before and after they came into the war, to predispose French North Africa to them, to have the closest observation of the country, to have a strong footing there, and to make all kinds of contacts with all kinds of people, especially important military and civil functionaries. When we began to plan this expedition with them they redoubled their efforts not only to acquire information and to create good will, but also to make a regular conspiracy among the high French officers there to come over with their troops to the Allies, should an American landing take place.

Great Britain is supposed in American circles to be very unpopular with the French. I do not think it is true, and certainly our troops have had the very best reception in Northwest Africa once we got ashore. Nevertheless, as we had been firing on the French on so many different occasions and in so many places, it was not worth while to contest the point. The whole enterprise therefore was organized on the basis not only of American command but of having Americans everywhere in evidence at the crucial moment of landing. If you keep in your mind the supreme object, namely, the destruction of Hitler and Hitlerism, there is no room for small points of national self-assertiveness. As long as the job is done, it does not matter much who gets the credit. We have no need to be anxious about the place which our country will occupy in the history of this war, nor, when the facts are known, about the part which we have played in the great enterprise called TORCH.

I now turn to examine a peculiar form of French mentality, or rather of the mentality of a large proportion of Frenchmen in the terrible defeat and ruin which has overtaken their country. I am not at all defending or still less eulogizing this French mentality. But it would be very foolish not to try to understand what is passing in other people's minds and what are the secret springs of action to which they respond. The Almighty in His infinite wisdom did not see fit to create Frenchmen in the image of Englishmen. In a state like France, which has experienced so many convulsions—Monarchy, Convention, Directory, Consulate, Empire, Monarchy, Empire, and finally Republic—there has grown up a principle founded on the *droit administratif* which undoubtedly governs the action of many French officers and officials in times of revolution and change. It is a highly legalistic habit of mind and it arises from a subconscious sense of national self-preservation against the dangers of sheer anarchy. For instance, any officer who obeys the command of his lawful superior or of one whom he believes to be his lawful superior is absolutely immune from subsequent punishment. Much, therefore, turns in the minds of French officers upon whether there is a direct, unbroken chain of lawful command, and this is held to be more important by many Frenchmen than moral, national, or international considerations. From this point of view many Frenchmen who admire General de Gaulle and envy him in his role nevertheless regard him as a man who has rebelled against the authority of the French state, which in their prostration they conceive to be vested in the person of the antique defeatist who to them is the illustrious and venerable Marshal Pétain, the hero of Verdun and the sole hope of France.

Now, all this may seem very absurd to our minds. But there is one aspect about it which is important to us. It is in accordance with orders and authority transmitted or declared to be transmitted by Marshal Pétain that the French troops in Northwest Africa have pointed and fired their rifles against the Germans and Italians instead of continuing to point and fire their rifles against the British and Americans. I am sorry to have to mention a point like that, but it makes a lot of difference to a soldier whether a man fires his gun at him or at his enemy; and even the soldier's wife or father might have a feeling about it, too.

It was the opinion of those officers who were ready to come over to our side that any admixture of de Gaullist troops at the outset would destroy all hope of a peaceful landing. Although we were prepared to bear down all opposition and in fact did overcome a very considerable degree of opposition, it is my duty to confess that neither we nor the Americans were looking for additional trouble, there being quite enough going about at the present time. The Americans, who, as I have said, were in command from the beginning, for their part refused to allow the slightest intervention of de Gaullists into this theater.

There was, however, one French figure upon whom our hopes were set—General Giraud—a very senior French officer who was taken prisoner before the French surrender in 1940 while fighting gallantly in a tank and who a few months ago made his second remarkable and dramatic escape from German captivity. Giraud is an undoubted hero of the French Army. General Juin, who commanded the important Algiers garrison and Army Corps, was ready to act as his lieutenant. From our point of view there was nothing wrong with General Giraud. We, therefore, at General Eisenhower's request, sent a British submarine under the American flag to cruise off the French Riviera coast and on the night of November 6, two days before the dawn of zero, we picked up the General, took him out to sea, transferred him to a seaplane, and brought him to Gibraltar, where he arrived on the afternoon of the seventh. We all thought General Giraud was the man for the job and that his arrival would be electrical. In this opinion General Giraud emphatically agreed and he made the most sweeping demands for plenary authority to be given to him as Supreme Commander-in-Chief of all the forces in or ever to be brought into Northwest Africa. Some hours passed in persuading him to reduce these claims to the bounds of reason.

Under the influence of General Juin, Algiers surrendered on the evening of the eighth. By the afternoon of the ninth, General Clark had established Allied Advanced Headquarters there. Here was found Admiral Darlan, who had been in our hands, though treated with all consideration since the day before. He had come back after his official tour to visit his son, who is said to be dying.

The landing at Casablanca was proceeding very slowly in the face of obstinate opposition. Large numbers of ships crammed with troops were lolling about outside the range of the forts and the U-boats were arriving on the scene in ever-increasing numbers. On four days out of five off Casablanca the surf is too great for landing on the beaches. The Americans had hitherto been astonishingly favored by fortune in the weather, but it might have broken at any moment, and, if so, the greater part of the armada off Casablanca would have to crowd into the bay at Gibraltar or go on cruising about in the open sea among the U-boats. Although Oran capitulated on the tenth, the landing facilities there would have been wholly insufficient to deal except very slowly with double the force which we had already assigned for it. Indecisive and protracted operations in this area would have put a peculiar stress on Spain, whose interests were affected and whose fears and appetites alike might easily have been excited. It was therefore of the utmost importance to bring the fighting at Casablanca to a close as soon as possible. Of course, looking back on all these events after they have turned out right, it is not easy to recall how hazardous they looked to us, to the American Chiefs of the Staff, or to General Eisenhower beforehand and while they were going on. The United States might have lost ten thousand to twenty thousand men drowned by U-boats apart from the fighting on the beaches and the fire of the harbor batteries. Moreover, the need for speed in the whole campaign was intensely felt by us all.

Morocco and Algeria were only steppingstones to the real prize, which is Tunisia, which held and holds the key to the central Mediterranean. To get eastward with the utmost rapidity was only possible if the French would not only cease fighting, but would abstain from sabotaging railways and roads and actively assist in unloading the ships. Delay in getting eastward would give the Germans the time to fly and ferry over a powerful army, and every day lost might mean a week's heavy fighting with thousands of extra casualties. This was the situation on the tenth with which General Clark at Algiers and his superior General Eisenhower at Gibraltar had to deal.

All the high French authorities in Tunis, Algeria, and Morocco had been invited to Algiers, and most of them had complied. Darlan, Giraud, Juin, Noguës, Châtel, and various others were gathered. Admiral Esteva, in whom we had great hopes, was held in Bizerta by the enemy. These Frenchmen wrangled together in the most bitter manner. But under the vehement pressure of United States' General Clark for a decision one way or the other, Giraud and all the other French authorities present agreed to accept Darlan as their leader and custodian of the mystical authority of the Marshal and the honor of France. Darlan, although virtually a prisoner, at first refused to do anything, but eventually, late in the afternoon, he agreed to accept General Clark's terms and to send orders by air to stop all French resistance to the Allied forces. All fighting at Casablanca thereafter ceased, though whether as the result of Darlan's order is not known, and the heavy American disembarkations began. The provisional emergency agreement made in these circumstances by General Clark and Admiral Darlan was approved, for what it was worth, by General Eisenhower. This was the beginning of the relationship with Darlan.

Next day, the eleventh, another great event occurred. Hitler overran unoccupied France in the teeth of the protests of the venerable and illustrious Marshal. This constituted a breach of the armistice. The French officers considered themselves released from its conditions. All bets were off. There was a new deal. It could be said that the venerable and illustrious Marshal was no longer a free agent. His authority was therefore even more clearly held to reside in Admiral Darlan. Darlan was the only authority plainly derived from Marshal Pétain. General Giraud could not claim that authority. He had left France without the permission of Marshal Pétain and even, as was suggested, breaking his written promise to him. The remarkable thing is that General Giraud was himself impressed by the arguments of the other Frenchmen. He was quite soon convinced that he had no power whatever to influence the decision and, more than that, he seems to have felt himself at a disadvantage compared with these other Frenchmen who could prove they had obeyed the orders emanating legally from the head of the state.

On the thirteenth, General Eisenhower, with Admiral Cunningham, arrived at Algiers from Gibraltar for the first time and began more formal conversations with General Clark, Admiral Darlan, General Giraud, and other French high officers. His object now was not merely to obtain a cessation of resistance but to bring the whole French military and administrative machine actively over to our side.

On the fourteenth, he telegraphed to the Combined Chiefs of Staff in Washington under whom he is serving that he had reached an agreement with the Frenchmen; that they would accept only Darlan's leadership and that Darlan would co-operate with the Allied army. The main point was that General Eisenhower recognized Admiral Darlan as the supreme French authority in Northwest Africa. This was not a treaty. It was an arrangement made by the American Commander-in-Chief in the field with the local authorities to facilitate the safe landing of his troops and the eastward movement of his army. Not only all the American generals but Admiral Cunningham, who knows the Mediterranean from end to end and who had been in the TORCH enterprise for several months, and also the representatives of the Foreign Office and the State Department who were present, strongly urged acceptance of the subsequent written agreement by their governments. All the French forces and officials came over to our side, thus relieving the Americans of the anxieties and difficulties which a forcible taking over of the administration of these vast regions would have imposed upon them and us, and of the still more imminent risk of sabotage of our communications to the eastward. Giraud was appointed by Darlan Commander-in-Chief and hastened to rally the French troops to their new allegiance. The French garrison in Tunis, who had made no resistance to the German landings, which had already begun there, marched out of the city to the westward and took up positions facing east against the Germans. Fraternization ensued between the British, American, and French soldiers. The populace, whose sympathies were never in doubt, but who in some places seemed sunk in coma and in bewilderment, became enthusiastic, and the whole enterprise proceeded with speed and vigor. So much for what happened on the spot.

In these emergency transactions His Majesty's government had not been consulted in any way; nor did we know the details of all the violent events which were happening. The decision which the President had to take was whether to disavow or endorse what his General had done. He backed him up. The question before us was whether we should repudiate General Eisenhower at the risk of a very serious break with the United States. I have no doubt whatever that we should have been very careless of the lives of our men and of the interests of the common cause if we had done anything of the kind. However, on November 17 I telegraphed to the President in the following sense:

I ought to let you know that very deep currents of feeling are stirred by the arrangement with Darlan. The more I reflect upon it the more convinced I become that it can only be a temporary expedient justifiable solely by the stress of battle. We must not overlook the serious political injury which may be done to our cause, not only in France but throughout Europe, by the feeling that we are ready to make terms with the local Quislings. A permanent arrangement with Darlan or the formation of a Darlan government in French North Africa would not be understood by the great masses of ordinary people whose simple loyalties are our strength.

My own feeling is that we should get on with the fighting and let that overtake the parleys, and we are all very glad to hear that General Eisenhower expects to be able to order the leading elements of our First Army to attack the Germans in Tunis and Bizerta in the course of the next few days.

On this the President a few hours later made the statement to his press conference which was published and gave so much general satisfaction. To me he telegraphed at midnight on the seventeenth the text of the statement he had just given out at his press conference:

I have accepted General Eisenhower's political arrangements for the time being in Northern and Western Africa. I thoroughly understand and approve the feeling in the United States and Great Britain, and among all the other United Nations, that in view of the history of the past two years no permanent arrangement should be made with Admiral Darlan. People in the United Nations likewise would never understand the recognition of a reconstituting of the Vichy government in France or in any

French territory. We are opposed to Frenchmen who support Hitler and the Axis.

No one in our Army has any authority to discuss the future government of France and the French Empire. The future French government will be established—not by any individual in metropolitan France or overseas—but by the French people themselves after they have been set free by the victory of the United Nations. The present temporary arrangement in North and West Africa is only a temporary expedient, justified solely by the stress of battle.

The present temporary arrangement has accomplished two military objectives. The first was to save American and British lives on the one hand and French lives on the other hand. The second was the vital factor of time. The temporary arrangement has made it possible to avoid a "mopping up" period in Algiers and Morocco which might have taken a month or two to consummate. Such a period would have delayed the concentration for the attack from the west on Tunis, and we hope on Tripoli.

Every day of delay in the current operation would have enabled the Germans and Italians to build up a strong resistance, to dig in and make a huge operation on our part essential before we could win. Here again, many more lives will be saved under the present speedy offensive than if we had had to delay it for a month or more. It will also be noted that French troops under the command of General Giraud have already been in action against the enemy in Tunisia, fighting by the side of American and British soldiers for the liberation of their country. Admiral Darlan's proclamation assisted in making a "mopping up" period unnecessary. Temporary arrangements made with Admiral Darlan apply, without exception, to the current local situation only. I have requested the liberation of all persons in Northern Africa who had been imprisoned because they opposed the efforts of the Nazis to dominate the world, and I have asked for the abrogation of all laws and decrees inspired by Nazi governments or Nazi ideologists. Reports indicate that the French of North

Africa are subordinating all political questions to the formation of a common front against the common enemy.

It seemed to me that these statements by the President safeguard what I may call the long-term policy, and we should do very well to rest upon them. I must, however, say that personally I consider that in the circumstances prevailing General Eisenhower was right, and even if he was not quite right I should have been very reluctant to hamper or impede his action when so many lives and such vitally important issues hung in the balance. I do not want to shelter myself in any way behind the Americans or anyone else.

Now, how far are we committed to Admiral Darlan? There is no doubt that if you ask for a man's help and he gives it in a manner that is most valuable to you, on the faith of an agreement entered into amid dangers which are thereby relieved, you have contracted a certain obligation towards him. I do not want the House to have any illusions about this. Both governments had undoubtedly the right to reject General Eisenhower's agreement with Admiral Darlan, but in view of what had happened it is perfectly clear that a certain obligation had been contracted towards him. More than that, we had benefited greatly from the assistance we had received. I do not consider that any long-term or final agreement has been entered into. I do not consider that the agreement is a document to be interpreted by legalistic processes. It is a question of fair dealing, and of this General Eisenhower is in the first instance the judge. He states that he does not consider that he is in any way bound permanently to Admiral Darlan. He claims that he has the sole right of interpretation. Darlan and the other French leaders are certainly in his power, and I for my part hope that he will interpret his obligations in a reasonable and honorable manner, even to a man like Darlan.

Since then events have moved at a gallop. The American and British armies, several hundreds of thousands strong, with all their complicated and ponderous tackle, have now landed and are in control of the whole of French Northwest Africa, an area over nine hundred miles long from west to east, with the exception only of the twenty or thirty miles of the Tunisian tip on which the Germans and Italians are endeavoring to build up an array and where the Germans are desperately and vigorously resisting. The whole French Army and administration are working wholeheartedly on the side of the Allies. It is much too late for their leaders to turn back now. We need their aid, but they are in our power. The French troops have fought well on two occasions. On the first, six hundred of them repelled a German attack without yielding an inch of ground, although they suffered twenty-five per cent casualties. On the second, supported by United States artillery and some parachutists, they destroyed a German battle group at Faid and took the position together with one hundred prisoners, mostly German. They are guarding a long line from about forty miles south of the Mediterranean down to the Tripolitanian frontier, holding back the German and Italian patrols and pressing forward as far as their strength allows towards Sfax and Gabès. As our troops come up we shall reinforce them strongly. Meanwhile Admiral Darlan succeeded in bringing the whole of French West Africa, including the key strategic base of Dakar, to our side against the enemy. I asked the President whether I might refer to certain secret telegrams and I have just received the following from him:

> You might add from me if you wish that General Eisenhower has definite instructions from me to enter into no agreement or bilateral contract with Admiral Darlan, but that all decisions by Eisenhower shall be unilateral on our part, and shall take the form of announcements from the military Commander-in-Chief of our Armed Forces. Furthermore, I hope you will call attention to the fact that Dakar, instead of being a menace, is today open to use by British and American ships and planes in the prosecution of the war.

The advantages of Dakar coming over are enormous, and saved us a costly and perhaps bloody expedition. We are to have all the facilities of the port. The United States deal for us in the matter; they have adopted the claims the Admiralty made and we are to share with them all these facilities. The powerful modern battleship *Richelieu* can go to the United States to be completed. Other French vessels are being formed into a squadron which obeys the orders of Admiral Darlan. Darlan is actively endeavoring through his emissaries to persuade Admiral Godfrey, who commands the French squadron interned in Alexandria Harbor, and is paid by us, to come out on our side. So far he has not succeeded, but we are hopeful. Questions of honor appear to be specially complicated in this case.

All this is done in the sacred name of the Marshal, and when the Marshal bleats over the telephone orders to the contrary and deprives Darlan of his nationality, the Admiral rests comfortably upon the fact or fiction, it does not much matter which, that the Marshal is acting under the duress of the invading Hun, and that he, Darlan, is still carrying out his true wishes. In fact, if Admiral Darlan had to shoot Marshal Pétain he would no doubt do it in Marshal Pétain's name.

While all this has been going on, Admiral Darlan was naturally somewhat affected by the President's outspoken declaration and other statements which reached his ears. It may be of interest to hear a letter which he wrote to General Clark. We are not called upon to approve or sympathize with his position, but it is just as well to understand it:

Monsieur le Général,

Information from various sources tends to substantiate the view that "I am only a lemon which the Americans will drop after they have squeezed it dry."

In the line of conduct which I have adopted out of pure French patriotic feeling, in spite of the serious disadvantages which it entails for me, at the moment when it was extremely easy for me to let events take their course without my intervention, my own personal position does not come into consideration.

I acted only because the American government has solemnly undertaken to restore the integrity of French sovereignty as it existed in 1939, and because the armistice between the Axis and France was broken by the total occupation of metropolitan France, against which the Marshal has solemnly protested.

I did not act through pride, ambition, nor calculation, but because the position which I occupied in my country made it my duty to act.

When the integrity of France's sovereignty is an accomplished fact—and I hope that it will be in the least possible time—it is my firm intention to return to private life and to end my days, in the course of which I have ardently served my country, in retirement.

During the last summer I have established close and friendly relations with General Eisenhower. I do not think I can give a better general picture of the situation than the latest message which he has sent to me. It was dispatched on December 5:

In the political field it is easily evident that our war communications system has not served us well in trying to keep you fully informed. This has been aggravated by the fact that difficulties in censorship here have permitted rumors to go out that have no foundation in truth. Among these stories is one that the American military authorities are dealing with Darlan about matters that have nothing to do with the local military situation, and are supporting his claims to a permanent authority rather than as merely the temporary head of the local government. Nothing could be further from the fact. Admiral Cunningham, Mr. Mack, Brigadier Whiteley, and other British officers are kept closely and intimately informed of all moves made, both in our local dealings with Darlan and in the weary process we have been going through in straightening out the Dakar tangle. At every meeting with Darlan, I tell him that so far as this headquarters is concerned, he is at the head of a local *de facto* organization by means of which we are enabled to secure the co-operation, both military and civil, that we need for the prosecution of this campaign. He knows I am not empowered to go further than this.

I assure you again that we are not entering a cabal designed to place Darlan at the head of anything except the local organization. Here he is entirely necessary, for he and he alone is the source of every bit of practical help we have received. If you will contemplate the situation existing along our lines of communication, which extend five hundred miles from here through mountainous country to Tunisia, you will understand that the local French could, without fear of detection, so damage us that we would have to retreat hurriedly back to ports from which we could supply ourselves by sea. Giraud quickly gave up trying to help us and it was only through Darlan's help that we are now fighting the Boche in Tunisia instead of somewhere in the vicinity of Bône or even west of that. It appears to us that both Boisson and Darlan are committed irrevocably to an Allied victory....

The military prospects depend upon several factors, of which the most important is our ability to build up fighter cover for our ground troops. This, in turn, depends upon getting supplies, establishing forward fields, and maintaining a rapid flow of fighter craft until the battle is won. It depends also upon weather, until we can get steel mats on all our mud fields. The next thing we must do is to get forward every available scrap of ground reinforcement and replacements for troops now on the line, who need a short rest. In addition, we must get our communication lines to work so well that all ground and air troops will be assured of adequate reserves when more intensive fighting starts again. The third great factor is our ability to prevent rapid reinforcement by the enemy. Our bombing fields are now so far removed from targets that the scale of our air bombing is not what we should like, but we are doing our best. Finally, during all this we must provide adequate protection for our land and sea lines of communication, especially our ports. All these jobs strain our resources and keep everyone going at top speed, but we shall yet get them done. But all this shows you how dependent we are upon French passive and active co-operation and, so far, we have no evidence of reluctance on Darlan's part to help us.

It is very necessary that the two governments and, if I

may say so, the President and I, keep very closely together, as we are doing. After all, what is it we want? We want the maximum possible united French effort against the common enemy. This, I believe, can be achieved, but it can only be achieved gradually and it will best be achieved by the action of Frenchmen. If Admiral Darlan proceeds to render important services, he will undoubtedly deserve consideration in spite of his record, but that consideration gives him no permanent claims even upon the future of the French possessions which have rallied to him, still less upon the future of France.

The Germans by their oppression will soon procure for us the unity of metropolitan France. That unity can now only take an anti-German form. In such a movement the spirit of the Fighting French must be continually in the ascendant. Their reward will come home on the tide. We must try to bring about as speedily as possible a working arrangement and ultimately a consolidation between all Frenchmen outside the German power. The character and constitution of Admiral Darlan's government must be continuously modified by the introduction of fresh and, from our point of view, clean elements. We have the right and I believe we have the power to effect these necessary transformations so long as Great Britain and the United States act harmoniously together. But meanwhile, above all, let us get on with the war.

I must say I think he is a poor creature with a jaundiced outlook and disorganized loyalties who in all this tremendous African episode, west and east alike, can find no point to excite his interest except the arrangements made between

General Eisenhower and Admiral Darlan. The struggle for the Tunisian tip is now rising to its climax and the main battle impends. Another trial of strength is very near on the frontiers of Cyrenaica. Both these battles will be fought almost entirely by soldiers from this island. The 1st and 8th British Armies will be engaged to the full. I cannot take my thoughts away from them and their fortunes, and I expect that will be the feeling of the House of Commons.

The House will, I believe, feel that it is being well and faithfully served by His Majesty's government. I ask them to support us in refusing to do anything at this juncture which might add to the burdens and losses of our troops. I ask them to give their confidence to the government and to believe in their singleness and inflexibility of purpose. I ask them to treat with proper reprobation that small, busy and venomous band who harbor and endeavor to propagate unworthy and unfounded suspicions, and so to come forward unitedly with us in all the difficulties through which we are steadfastly and successfully making our way.